STARTLEMENT

ALSO BY ADA LIMÓN

POETRY
The Hurting Kind
The Carrying
Bright Dead Things
Sharks in the Rivers
This Big Fake World
Lucky Wreck

EDITOR
You Are Here

CHILDREN'S BOOKS
And, Too, the Fox, illustrated by Gaby D'Alessandro
In Praise of Mystery, illustrated by Peter Sís

STARTLEMENT

NEW AND SELECTED POEMS

ADA LIMÓN

corsair poetry

CORSAIR

First published in the United States in 2025 by Milkweed Editions
First published in Great Britain in 2026 by Corsair

1 3 5 7 9 10 8 6 4 2

Copyright © Ada Limón, 2025

The moral right of the author has been asserted.

*All characters and events in this publication, other than those
clearly in the public domain, are fictitious and any resemblance
to real persons, living or dead, is purely coincidental.*

All rights reserved.
No part of this publication may be reproduced, stored in a
retrieval system, or transmitted, in any form or by any means, without
the prior permission in writing of the publisher, nor be otherwise circulated
in any form of binding or cover other than that in which it is published
and without a similar condition including this condition being
imposed on the subsequent purchaser.

A CIP catalogue record for this book
is available from the British Library.

Hardback ISBN: 978-1-4721-6065-2

Printed and bound in Great Britain by Clays Ltd, Elcograf S.p.A.

Papers used by Corsair are from well-managed forests
and other responsible sources.

Corsair	The authorised representative
An imprint of	in the EEA is
Little, Brown Book Group	Hachette Ireland
Carmelite House	8 Castlecourt Centre
50 Victoria Embankment	Dublin 15, D15 XTP3, Ireland
London EC4Y 0DZ	(email: info@hbgi.ie)

An Hachette UK Company
www.hachette.co.uk

www.littlebrown.co.uk

For Lucas & for the Earth

CONTENTS

from **LUCKY WRECK**

First Lunch with Relative Stranger Mister You · 3
Little Day · 6
A Little Distantly, As One Should · 7
This Darkness · 11
The Echo Sounder · 12
Farmers' Almanac · 16
Miles Per Hour · 18
The Firemen Are Dancing · 20
Little Monogamy · 21
The Unbearable · 22
The Spider Web · 23
The Lessing Table · 30
All Kinds of Shipwrecks · 31
Centerfold · 32
The Frontier of Never Leaving · 33

from **THIS BIG FAKE WORLD**

Prologue: This Big Fake World · 37
He Wishes for Things Smaller · 38
His Wife Was Not Something He Could Hang on the Tree · 40
Ideal Fire · 41
On a Business Trip He Contemplates Her Closet · 42
After Her Husband Left Her, She Went to Work at the
    Hardware Store · 43
At the Hardware Store · 44
The Note He Does Not Leave · 45
He Has Big Thoughts While His Wife Is Sleeping · 46
The Hardware Lady Repeats Herself · 47
He Renames the House After His Own · 48

Our Hero Sits at Home Alone and So Does the Hardware Lady · 49
The Hardware Lady Watches as Our Hero Comes Close · 51
Epilogue: This Big Fake World · 52

from **SHARKS IN THE RIVERS**

Sharks in the Rivers · 55
Flood Coming · 57
Diagnosis: Even the Stillaguamish River Cannot Stop Time · 58
Overjoyed · 59
Crush · 60
The New World of Beauty · 61
The Russian River · 63
Marketing Life for Those of Us Left · 64
Hardworking Agreement with a Wednesday · 66
Homesick · 68
Ways to Ease Your Animal Mind · 69
The Crossing · 70
The Same Thing · 72
Bird Bound for a Good World · 74
Drowning in Paradise · 76
To the Busted Among Us · 77

from **BRIGHT DEAD THINGS**

How to Triumph Like a Girl · 81
During the Impossible Age of Everyone · 82
The Last Move · 83
How Far Away We Are · 85
The Quiet Machine · 86
I Remember the Carrots · 87
Someplace Like Montana · 88
State Bird · 90
Downhearted · 91

What It Looks Like to Us and the Words We Use · 92
Cower · 93
Relentless · 94
The Riveter · 96
After You Toss Around the Ashes · 98
Torn · 99
Adaptation · 100
The Conditional · 101

from THE CARRYING

Ancestors · 105
The Leash · 106
The Raincoat · 107
The Vulture & the Body · 108
Dandelion Insomnia · 110
Dead Stars · 111
What I Want to Remember · 113
Overpass · 115
Wonder Woman · 116
The Real Reason · 117
The Year of the Goldfinches · 119
Sundown & All the Damage Done · 120
A New National Anthem · 121
The Contract Says: We'd Like the Conversation to Be Bilingual · 123
Instructions on Not Giving Up · 125
Carrying · 126
What I Didn't Know Before · 127
Love Poem with Apologies for My Appearance · 128
Losing · 129
The Last Drop · 130

from THE HURTING KIND

Give Me This · 133
Sanctuary · 134
A Good Story · 135
Forsythia · 136
And, Too, the Fox · 137
The Magnificent Frigatebird · 138
The First Fish · 139
Joint Custody · 140
Cyrus & the Snakes · 141
Calling Things What They Are · 143
Open Water · 144
Privacy · 145
Sports · 146
Proof · 148
Heart on Fire · 149
My Father's Mustache · 150
The Hurting Kind · 151
Against Nostalgia · 158
Salvage · 159
The End of Poetry · 160

STARTLEMENT | NEW POEMS

The Endlessness · 163
Hell or High Water · 164
While Everything Else Was Falling Apart · 166
Strange Refuge · 167
This One Goes Out To · 169
Field · 171
Mortality · 172
Sea Turtle · 173
Crow's-Feet · 175

Let Loose · 176
How to Measure Distance · 177
Literary Theory · 182
Even Here It Is Happening · 183
The Geography of Mountains · 184
Curtain Call · 187
Every Blooming Thing · 190
On Earth as It Is on Earth · 191
In the End, Everything Gives · 192
Startlement · 194
The Origin Revisited · 195
In Praise of Mystery: A Poem for Europa · 197

Notes on New Poems · 199
Acknowledgments for New Poems · 201

Not knowing when the Dawn will come,
I open every Door.

—EMILY DICKINSON

STARTLEMENT

from LUCKY WRECK

FIRST LUNCH WITH RELATIVE STRANGER MISTER YOU

We solved the problem of the wind
                               with an orange.

Now we've got the problem
                             of the orange.

Jimmy once said, *Do you get along with everyone*
                             as good as this?

I did not know how to say yes.

In Albuquerque yes is hard/easy/look
                             a roadrunner!

You there, across the table, could be my opposite
of enemy. I do not want 8 babies.

Are you hooked on height?

I'm trying to stop myself from telling you
about the time I lost my passport

and so thought of killing myself,
identity being an important instrument
of my behavior.

I saved myself by thinking I'd write a novel
and then fell asleep in the closet.

It's called, the novel, *Last Things for Lala*.

It is not called, *The Contradictory Nature of Hangers*.

What is the punctum?

Out of which limb will you grow?

Jimmy had two sons, nice ones.
Two taller than me. I bought them food and listened
to ICP in the '65 Chevy.

I was 53 years old. That's one year older than Jimmy.

I've never been where you live,
but that doesn't mean I should move there.

I get attached to rocks.

At the tone the time will be: *Let's never die!*

We've just met, should we move to Ensenada?

Or should I just borrow a pen?

I could tie your shoelaces

                together and play king

of the mountain.

I've brought a lot to the table.

You've brought an orange.

I'd rather sit a kiss than you would.

My fist is like a kiss.

I want a shirt that says, Kiss Me or I'll Cut You.

I want to start every sentence with,
>
> *Let me tell you something, Mister.*

Mister who smells like yellow.

> Mister who has too many pockets.
>
> > Mister who is a Mister times two,
> >
> > > Mister who misses and then gets sad,
> > >
> > > > Mister whose lunch I'm having.

What to do with the problem of the orange?

Let me tell you something Mister,

> you've got to peel it.

LITTLE DAY

This is what it comes down to:
Me on a park bench, always writing,
This is what it comes down to.

A LITTLE DISTANTLY, AS ONE SHOULD

I.

I keep wanting to write about
accidents and how I hate them and it's so
obvious. Everyone hates accidents.

So, instead I've been watching
my neighbors set up their picnic table
and tent (do you call it a cabana?).
The man is wearing a bandana
and a leather vest without a shirt, a look
I've never learned to appreciate,
even though I am from California.
The woman looks like that bartender Kim,
but younger. I've overheard that they're
expecting company in approximately 45 minutes.
I have noted the time. I'm excited for them.

It's hard to be excited for things,
not the same way as I used to, or maybe
it's just that I don't get stoned anymore.
Jake and I listened to a Neil Young album
in my old apartment over and over
again for hours. Every time I tell someone
that he's died, that same image pops into my head.
He's sitting on the windowsill with the light
behind him so you can't see his face.
I'm very aware that he's younger than me.
He wasn't stoned. Jake was a good kid.

My friend, all the time, says *I'm so excited*,
and when I ask her, for what, she just shrugs
and says, *Aren't you?* I suppose so. Yes.

2.

Up on a mountain near Lake Tahoe,
I once fell in love with a boy named
Billy, or was it Bobby? I was thirteen
and he was humoring me. I needed humoring.
We had driven to the campground
in a huge blue station wagon my dad
had rented on account of our gear.
It felt unsafe. Station wagons for all their air
of safety always feel unsafe to me.
The way nuclear family should sound
comforting and yet it only ever sounds
like something that's going to explode.

If you've ever driven to Lake Tahoe
you know the roads. Long curving
gray snakes of pavement edged by
mountains and those drop-offs.
I hated them, still do. But when you have to
get somewhere you drive on them.
(I have to tell myself this all the time.)
You can't really stop going places
because you're frightened.

It's like that road sign that's the image
of rocks falling down a mountain
onto the road. I never knew what you were
supposed to do about that, duck?
Is it saying that inevitably a rock will
fall on you? Is this good that we know this?

I am obviously unsure of the usefulness
of inevitable things. Even the word
inevitable is awkward and hard to spell.

I never kissed Bobby or anything,
although I probably should have.

3.

Sometimes I think the memory of an event
is better than the event itself. The way
the retelling of something is satisfying.
That's why it's so unsettling when I can't
remember everything in detail.

I want to remember the exact song
that my brother and I were singing
in the back seat of that rented station wagon.
All that I keep thinking of is "Respect"
by Aretha Franklin. I can't imagine
that's what we were singing, but maybe
that's why it stands out. It was unusual,
like the car and the roads.
I can convince myself of anything.

My neighbors (the *my* there is so endearing,
it makes me love them) have finished
with their cabana and the Kim lady is power washing
the chairs. They are laughing and getting
along well. She doesn't mind his vest.

Now, I am almost positive it was "Respect."
Seeing them in print can help the facts become fact.

When I think about it, I would like to go back
to Lake Tahoe when it's warm out and swim.
That's where Jake was when he died.
The car went off one of those roads
I mentioned earlier. (I was going to tell you then,
but it was strange to write it down.)

But now, the guests have arrived!
(They were 21 minutes late.) The vest is lighting
the barbecue and one woman is pregnant
and in overalls. The whole thing is so domestic
and soft you can almost wear it.

4.

I have gone out to the fire escape
and come back now to my desk. I wanted
to be there with the neighbors for a while.
The Kim lady waved and I waved back,
a little distantly, as one should, as if
I cared only a little, as if they were only a fleeting
thought and me, simply a body on a windowsill
passing through.

THIS DARKNESS

This darkness is not the scary one,
it's the one before the sun comes up,
the one you can still breathe in.

THE ECHO SOUNDER

> echo sounder *n. A device for measuring depth of water by sending pressure waves down from the surface and recording the time until the echo returns from the bottom.* —AMERICAN HERITAGE DICTIONARY

1.

She enters the world a ready-set-go girl.
She comes with a list of things she cannot
see, she comes with a language restricted
by its own inability to name things
as she sees them. She believes that there are two
worlds and she lives in the one that is
separate from the other, the seed that comes
up outside the garden, the one door with no
handle, the shingle in the roof with the
weathervane, the arrow flying from the quiver,
the child who can balance on her palms
and is hated for it. She wears no shirt,
still no one speaks to her. She speaks to
everyone. She has a bicycle and a family,
but it does not matter. She is difficult to
catch, she knows all the names of all the
fish, she is aware of them dying all the time,
upstream, the sockeye and the coho,
upstream, the Chinook and the king,
upstream, to the sand and rock nest of their
deaths. She thinks the bodies decay too quickly.

2.

When she is eleven years old, she thinks
her body will be like that of a fish. She does
not want to decay before she uses it.
She is confused in the dark. She is never
scared. She is convinced that she can talk
to God and she asks him a question.
She does not get an answer, so
she makes one up. She believes the answer is:
everything stops, the food is in the mouth,
but the mouth is not there,
the water flows, but there is no creek.
She understands now that bodies can swing
from trees and whole families can be
locked up, that people die the way fish do
starving sometimes, gutted and tortured
by children who think they are being
scientific and responsible. She thinks God
must know this and therefore he is ugly.
She decides God is no good, but he must exist,
he must exist so she can hold him accountable.
She decides this and then forgets.

3.

At one point she decides she is in love,
the way she woke one day and thought
she had dreamt up the word *Philadelphia*,
that there was no other word in the world
as beautiful as *Philadelphia* and how
she planned to make it mean something,
like the way everything can
touch you at once, the mason on the billboard,

the old theater's neon sign,
the water towers next to the cross,
the curve in the road where the school bus
stopped, the wet smell of boots and dirt,
the feeling when all those things get to you
and you want to cry or pray and because
you're no good at either, you
tell everyone to leave you alone so you
can go on feeling the world climbing around
in your body like you were just as much
a part of it as it was of you, maybe, she thought,
she could call that feeling *Philadelphia*.
She fell in love the same way.

4.

One week she thinks about offering,
how it is difficult to offer something of yourself.
She thinks it should be easy, how she
has an echo chamber in her chest. What
she sends out should reflect and return.
She goes to the creek on one
trip home and sits there for longer
than she planned. She decides to estimate
how long she will live and then she says
this is when she will die. She says it again,
This is when I will die, as if the repetition
will endow the words with nonsense, the way
a word becomes no longer a word, but a strange
sound that animals make, she takes comfort
in her animal-ness. She wants to go on
being an animal, not something that represents
something else, but the original object,

the thing before it is named, the fish before she knew it was a fish, when it was just another lost thing, individual and shadowy, working its way toward its own end.

FARMERS' ALMANAC

According to the *Farmers' Almanac* the best day to slaughter animals
is the 25th of this month. And all my horoscope said today was,
                                    Hooray for the differently sane!

The country I occupy is different than yours, but we both pretended
the vegetable steamer was a spaceship at one point or another
        and watched it real-fly to the kitchen.

My brother once pounded nails into the wood garden fence in the shape
of a hot rod. And then drove a hot rod in it. It was a hot rod inside a hot rod
        and I fell in love with men forever.

You there, I am collapsing, is it as
adorable as it feels?

Sincerity is what my meal is made out of.
        July 1st will be the best day to eat a meal of sincerity.

At the dinner table I still sit on my knees, like I'm praying,
        all the time, for more trouble.

One thousand toothpicks represent one thousand soldiers
        in the child's history report.

One thousand toothpicks represent only one thousand toothpicks
        in this report

but they still cannot stop gravity
from burying the things it tugs.

According to the *Farmers' Almanac*, this month, I am one more than falling down,
I am down falling,
I am catch-less.

To manage to miss things is an improbable act, to refer to people as things proves that I miss more of myself than others.

According to the *Farmers' Almanac* the master of invisibility finds himself dining, too often, alone.

In my country exploding things come from the inside like a sparkler and everyone notices and wants to warm

their hands on your burning body.

If I meet you again, let's make inappropriate sounds
all over town and by inappropriate I mean the sounds
                                        of our names.

MILES PER HOUR

The painted tiles are riddled with blue
cornflowers and unnaturally green stems,
as unnatural as trying to concentrate
on the blossoms covering the bathroom walls,
the way when we were driving 66 miles per hour,
and each lupine had become not one,
but rather one massive stain of purple and blue,
like one large bruise covering the right side
of Highway 12 and the more I tried
to find one leaf, one petal, the more dizzy
I became until the search for something
simple had ruined its way into nausea, into
that throbbing in the middle of my eyes
when we knew it was over, all of it and yet
we were still in the car, still going to meet
the family and when we pulled over on
Old Sonoma Road under the tree to make
love once more before the parental hand
shake made love more difficult, more
permanent, my head swelled not knowing
whether or not to hold onto the handle
or the stick shift or to shove my foot
on the dashboard or just to remain pinned
like that, pummeled in the car seat, what we called
screwing, the hard stuff, the times when we were more
angry than anything else, the turn-on being
the pain. And through the car window I could
see everything in summer heat, the oak leaves
the tires had crushed in their masculine heaviness,
the fungus that grew on the side of the tree making
a shape like a face or a birthmark and each single thing
made me grab you harder, want to be connected

to something larger, as if we could swell into
the universe itself, the movement of hips propelling
us up into some, I don't want to say celestial, body,
but something as big as that, where we could watch
over everything, the towns growing smaller like
little painted toys, those giant oaks and cedars,
turning into a brushstroke of blue and green, small
and unrecognizable as these flowers now, painted
haphazardly and scattered, like the memory
itself, the car driving farther and farther down
the highway, my face pressed up against the window
unable to discern whether or not I was as much
of a blur as the things I passed.

THE FIREMEN ARE DANCING

I am running my finger through the rough knotted hole
on the edge of the stained, oak, bar table.

It looks like it could be an eyehole and I think it
would be the scariest thing in the world if I were an ant,

a hole where the bottom drops out, just like that, onto the floor.

I don't want to drink tonight, or if I do, I want to drink a lot, enough
to lie down on the ash blackened floor and watch everything
through the eyehole.

Everyone is talking about parties, the vice cop keeps looking
at the guy we call Red and that's fine by me
because I don't like him, never have.

O and the firemen are dancing. My favorite part is how
they are dancing so close.

One is pulling the other to his hip and one with the hat is laughing
and tossing his head back as if they were seventeen or, even,
as if they were alone.

And it's okay that I don't have a specific *you* right now and it's okay
that I'm not sure who this *you* I am speaking to is anymore.

The firemen are dancing and one of them has leaned his head on the other's
blue shoulder and the ones at the window are singing
and watching with big, lovely, fireman smiles.

And it's okay that you weren't here to see it, I'm going to tell you
all about it. Even if you never ask, I will.

LITTLE MONOGAMY

This is done at a particular angle.
This is done level, done plumb.

I am no longer a public space.
I am worldwide to one.

THE UNBEARABLE

My grandmother only wants to tell me who died
and how. She tells me of all the traffic accidents
as if she was reading a menu to me out loud.
The man who was decapitated while driving
a tractor trying to make space for a new
Stop and Shop. The woman whose eyelashes
started growing inward until it was so painful
all she could do was lie there and scream and
then finally, not scream anymore. Over the kitchen
table I told her to stop it. She didn't
understand why it was making me upset.
It's what happens, and as she was trying to explain,
in my mind, I had already left the room and walked
up the street to the house I grew up in and laid
down outside on the green cement. In the shade
the cement was cool and hard. My old cat,
Smoke, came up and sat on my chest,
the way she never would when she was
alive, and in the trees there was a woodpecker
and squirrel bustling on their branches seeming very alien
and small. I have a friend who says that sometimes
when she thinks about animals she starts
to cry and right now even my dog is dying,
yesterday when someone was petting him,
he collapsed as if the weight of the hand was too much,
as if being touched, even in love, was unbearable.

THE SPIDER WEB

1.

The orb spider continues to spin a whole
Road map of a world on our large
Black living room window,
Each thread a highway to its charge.
The intricate lace of white lines stuck
Where a fly waits for his nip and his tuck.
It is so sturdy it will hardly ripple,
The house has to shake for it to shake even a little.
As the cars pass, it is solid as it is strobed.
Headlight after headlight, the same high beams
Run like upside down waves on the ceiling.
But the web holds the fly anxious for the final blow.
I watch as the spider comes close like a spy,
Unsure if I am jealous of the web or the fly.

2.

Unsure if I am jealous of the web or the fly,
Both of them sure of their beginnings and ends.
I slip into bed and lie there beside
Your body like a buoy that the ocean resents.
If I could just grab hold and find a way to paddle,
If you could stop dragging your feet along the gravel.
As a child I remember knowing how to float
When sober was the wind and my body, the boat.
Now each step is anchored and you continue to drift
In the room where we pretend that we are alive,
Where you and I commit the sin, and you and I forgive.
This is not holy but I wish the winds would shift,
Let some higher being take back the power,
As we mistreat our bodies, minute by minute, hour by hour.

3.

As we mistreat our bodies, minute by minute, hour by hour,
Day by day, the laundry piles up like driftwood and debris.
There is no coffee in the kitchen and the milk's gone sour.
I won't dust the living room so the spiders are free
To march in the corners and over piles of mail,
Like prisoners who've recently overthrown the jail.
Open a window, I can hear a voice in my head,
Get dressed. Get out. Wash the sheets on the bed.
It's not God, I tell you. It's my mother,
Though there is little difference between the two.
I'm convinced that together they're planning a coup.
She'll say I've got two problems, I'm one and you're the other.
She's right you know the tide is too high.
But we could drown in a glass of water, you and I.

4.

But we could drown in a glass of water, you and I,
Lying in this knee-deep pool of self-pity
With no intention of getting out or getting dry.
You argue that there is a freedom, a simplicity
In dropping beneath the usual swing of things.
But I am the one who keeps listening
When you start to speak as the television fades
And you begin your wallowing on the downside of day.
We must have some belief in this small life,
I still throw salt over my shoulder; you play the lottery.
There are nights when we make an effort to agree
And drift into bed where our bodies collide.
What would happen if we answered a letter or the phone?
Are we scared to discover that in fact, we are not alone?

5.

Are we scared to discover that in fact, we are not alone?
That the windows open out and the wind blows in,
That there is something familiar in this unknown
Need to protect our minds, our bodies, our skin,
And each other. You make me floss every night,
And worry now and then when I lose my appetite.
I want to lie down on your inconsistent shore,
Make myself a sandcastle and draw myself a door.
Come on, come out, or simply let me be
Alone and watch the waves pull their fingers back.
Instead, you hold me under until my body goes slack
In this living room sand by this suburban sea.
I've got no compass, no lifeboat, no mast, sail or stern,
Only the small prayer that, tomorrow, the tide will turn.

6.

Only the small prayer that, tomorrow, the tide will turn
And the net will come up full of feast has the hope
To break the silence in this house and make us unlearn
Our habits, our tracks or untie the knot in our rope.
Can a spider change his mind and cut the noose?
Can a fly lift her wings and pry herself loose?
Let's test the waters, drop the anchor, watch it sink
Into the waves the way you drop yourself in drink.
I will not enforce a curfew or try to hide your vice,
I may be blinded but I'm convinced we can stop,
Slow down, get right or simply watch the boat rock.
I will be the empty vessel and my heart the ice.
Pour something in me, the time is wasting.
I am the one doing the spinning and you, the tasting.

7.

I am the one doing the spinning and you, the tasting.
Your spinnerets spread your silk like a staysail-stay,
From my vantage point I can see the land erasing
Off the horizon and the night becoming day.
I'm not fighting anymore, tied to your mast
I am watching the web and the shadows it casts.
If I had my choice, I'd have a boat of my own,
The sails would be my skin, the bow my bones.
I'd paint a spider on the side and make it my omen,
Like a remembrance, a tattoo, of the life I left behind.
You could stay in this room with loathing on your mind,
I'd fly the flag and name her *Unmanned Woman*.
Still, I remain, trying to weave self-control
Where the orb spider continues to spin a hole.

THE LESSING TABLE

The dinner table was too small
and that was obvious.
We had to buy smaller forks,
smaller chairs, stop talking.

You took the saltshakers
off. I decided I'd only make
soft foods so we wouldn't have
to use knives anymore.

It kept on shrinking for days,
the butter taking over the dinner
plates, the green beans looking
longer and mean,

until it was just a thin slip
passed between us, a note
on blue-lined binder paper
in number two pencil:

Make the train wheels lock.
Make the mobile stop.
Do something, do something.

ALL KINDS OF SHIPWRECKS

The television is playing a show on shipwrecks,
and this voice is my favorite voice:

the voice that tells you where the treasure's hidden.
The structure of us is not a structure at all,

sleeping sideways on the foldout couch like visitors.
"We are not permanent here," the steel springs say,

and then the TV again, that sound so underwater smooth,
and how is it that they always find the wreck?

It is seven in the morning, another boat, another treasure.
Now, I am watching TV upside down, and what would I rather be:

the diver, or O lucky wreck to have been found?

CENTERFOLD

Crouched in the corner of the barn,
we sat with the cedar chest splayed,
and the magazines laid out in perfect
piles. I was the first to reach the
centerfold and together we stared.
These women, these giantesses,
folded over couches, on bear rugs,
or steel bars, their bodies so slick
they could slip through the pages
and then through your fingers.
One, in particular, was my favorite,
with her left leg perched on a ballet bar
and her hair piled around her shoulders,
I thought she must be famous.
I thought how lovely it would be to
be her, to be naked all the time,
and dancing.

THE FRONTIER OF NEVER LEAVING

If the wound you cover is made of sheet metal
and iron gates left over from the junkyard
of Forever Worried, and the school of Always Broken,
here, I have saved you a seat. If you have hidden your
outlawed books in your mattress and your outlawed
thoughts in your hands, here, I will give you refuge.
This is what I heard underneath it all, underneath and
in the beginning but now let's move to Canada. I hear it's nice
and they don't kill each other as often. I can even forgive them for speaking
French. Really, not all of them speak French. But would I miss it?
If I move to Canada and there's no war in the Spring,
I won't miss Iowa, that's for certain, but it's the only thing.
The fields keep growing longer like a veil between us,
the mountains like sutures on the map, and yet they are
ours, the way mustard can be ours off the highway
and windmills in the deserts and roads, even roads. Barbed
wire between us, fences between us. The roadrunner has
run into the river and Misters, you do not care. Another puzzle
piece of my American map has unfolded. I am the only
thing that fits together here, in this frontier of Never Leaving.
Today, I am going to play the record of the revolution,
everybody is going to sing along and the more we turn it up,
the less the flag will wave over you and the more it will
become a swallowtail and migrate to our houses, the little ones
in the back, the ones with the lights in the window. Look!
You can see them now, opening their doors in the fog.

from THIS BIG FAKE WORLD

PROLOGUE: THIS BIG FAKE WORLD

If this place that we live in includes
the kid with the chemicals and the lot
of old boats and carpet squares covered
with a sea of rocks from any given river,
wouldn't two people deserve to meet here,
somewhere down the street before the light
turns green, or before their hearts explode
from one dumb tragedy or another. I think so.
Give them that feeling like they have opened
all the envelopes and cleared off the kitchen
table to only the bare necessities, only
the stadium of themselves. Let the others
fall away like plastic figurines in a fish
bowl, their damage only superficial,
and let these small people rise up
and recover, let the man in the gray suit
be our hero for once, the woman
at the hardware store, the drunk,
and make each one of them remind us
that we have all come out of basic need,
some gnawing thing, some hunger.

HE WISHES FOR THINGS SMALLER

He is trying to make his love
smaller like a fist.

Of this he speaks to no one.

It is the same way he wished
to pray to something tiny—

some mouse-god, some bubble

blown from a fish's mouth.
O Mousy! O bubble!

Make this town collapse.

Make it fit into
a snow globe.

A snow globe he could do.

A snow globe he could manage,
and she'd be smaller too,

sitting in her car

at the light no longer
red. He could turn her

upside down and backward.

When he goes to the beach

he unfolds his folding
chair to face the parking lot.

This giant wave of nature
behind him, or rather, to which

he turns his back.

HIS WIFE WAS NOT SOMETHING HE COULD HANG ON THE TREE

On the way home from the party
he watched his wife hold the steering wheel
and thought he had never ridden
in the passenger seat before.

So many things he never noticed:
the old truck the Donaldsons decorated
in Christmas lights, how the clock
above Duncan's funeral parlor was still broken.

He couldn't remember giving her the keys,
or leaving the party, but he remembered
his friend Lewis, drunk and standing by the eggnog,
pointing out the women in their dresses, "Like live ornaments,"
Lewis said. "Except they're harder to break."

He watched his wife turn the corner
into the driveway. He knew she was
angry, but had given up on talking, her mouth
turned down like a fish's mouth awaiting
the hook, her hands releasing the wheel as if it was
the car that had disappointed her.

IDEAL FIRE

His wife said, "If you were a movie star,
you'd be Mark Harmon."

He got up then, left the door open
and walked down toward the river.

*Mark Harmon wasn't really
a movie star—and she knew it.*

He felt safe among the warehouses
with all their "wares" so useful.

One warehouse said IDEAL FIRE
in the color of wheelbarrow rust.

He thought it was strange
that what they made were fire

extinguishers. The "ideal fire"
being the fire one could easily put out.

ON A BUSINESS TRIP
HE CONTEMPLATES HER CLOSET

Flying back from Tulsa he realizes
he forgot his promise to take the various
small soaps and lotions from the
beige hotel room for his wife.

She collected them in case
of company. There was a closet
full of tiny white bottles and tiny
bars wrapped like tea cakes.

He was wondering if the company
she expected was particularly small,
and particularly dirty. But in truth,
he had never seen her put them to use.

She rearranged them constantly.
When coming home early he always
caught her hovering by the closet
and later when he peeked in, he noticed
they had all been dusted off and faced forward.

It was her own little army of cleanliness,
soldiers of good things and rules,
but lately it felt like it had a purpose.
She was building an arsenal against
a specific enemy, he thought,
and watched his city grow larger
as the plane began its descent.

AFTER HER HUSBAND LEFT HER, SHE WENT TO WORK AT THE HARDWARE STORE

When no one was in,
the store felt emptier than most
places a person could go.

A big key hung above the door
and cast a shadow like a crocodile
across the sunlit floor.

On the key was printed
KEY MADE HERE.
It was missing the S. She missed the S.

On a note pad by the register
she drew tiny squares absentmindedly,
while humming "Bargain Store"

by Dolly Parton. So many squares,
they began to look like small doors
through which one might slip.

AT THE HARDWARE STORE

The nails have been replaced
with miniature lighthouses
and snow globes.

She can barely manage
to sell paint; the souvenir
place-mats have won out.

Small glass ashtrays full of
small glass candy—not even
an ashtray's an ashtray anymore.

No one seems to notice nothing's
useful. She wants to buy a big box
of pencils and sharpen them.

Above the old HARDWARE sign
someone has scratched *hardly*
rather crookedly, but large and legible.

She likes the way it looks,
HARDLY HARDWARE.
It says what it means to say.
It does something, it fixes.

THE NOTE HE DOES NOT LEAVE

Our leading man is worried about the amount of nails he keeps buying from the lady at the hardware store. His garage is full of every kind of nail you could imagine, and he with nothing to fix, but maybe himself. He starts a note to his wife that he later crumples. It starts, "Being I have so many nails, I wish to be useful to someone."

HE HAS BIG THOUGHTS WHILE HIS WIFE IS SLEEPING

He thinks the moon is too
important tonight, too full
of itself; it likes to think
it can walk on water
or something.

But the moon has no allegiance
to anyone in this town,
like a hand on a snow globe
constantly shaking them up
and down.

THE HARDWARE LADY REPEATS HERSELF

She fingers the number 3 key
on the cash register without
noticing this strange woman, pretty

but limp, like a wet cat or
a dead bird, her eyes unfocused,
darting around like fleas.

Her cleaning supplies are all
lined up on the counter like weapons,
their nozzles pointing toward her.

The hardware lady is thinking
of a threesome she had in college
and runs her fingers over

a bowl of thumb tacks, skimming the surface,
avoiding the sharpest points.
Will that be all? she asks

and the woman nods, but
seems not to have heard her,
so again, *Will that be all?*

Then nothing, as if together,
they had already answered this question
one thousand times and finally
that had been enough.

HE RENAMES THE HOUSE AFTER HIS OWN

Now that she's gone, the sheets are days dirty
and he can smell when the earth moves in
through the window. The plastic plants lie
outside in the dumpster and seem to die there,
beautifully.

He bought a cardboard cup of coffee and
watched the ring form on the glass table;
it stayed there for days, he named it "Ringy,"
and when he cleaned it off he was almost sad,
honestly.

OUR HERO SITS AT HOME ALONE AND SO DOES THE HARDWARE LADY

1.

Tonight the radiator sounds like it's shuffling
cards out of boredom and of spite.

The woman outside is watching her shoes
as if they will run off and they might.

But it's okay—they're not very expensive.

This life is a fish story.

The sign on the window reads,
"This Window Opens," and it reads like
an invitation, not a warning.

(Open the window. This particular window.)

Tonight he's thinking that he's at the same time
stronger and weaker than most people.

2.

Across town she's thinking her life,
since the first incision, has only included
so much prodding by intruding strangers.

Things are never uniform the way she would
like them, laid out with instructions.
Most days, she'd give her right arm for
instructions and a decent paperback

and maybe a mouth with a song somewhere in it.

3.

There are two roads, two bridges, two, two, two.

The twos make sounds like plastic bells
all around the city, one cheap dull ring to another
dull ring.

4.

Precious things will come to them,
even in their simple wooden hour of
stillness.

He walks to the corner and is surprised
by a late snow fall, the sky endlessly giving.

5.

She thinks she can almost hear it,
the snow falling, deliberate proof
that even the sky wants to return and return
to this shattering world.

THE HARDWARE LADY WATCHES AS OUR HERO COMES CLOSE

This unknown yellow thing keeps rising
the way the horizon seems to find itself
again when the carnival ride ends and the
people get out of their lacquered compartments
to see the world, straight and permanent, lying there.
It is like that now as he hovers near
her counter, lingering, purposeful. The days have
made him bolder, his hands steady near
the cash register. She wants to ring him up.
She feels there is a safety in him, not
like the safety on a gun, but a safety
like a place you could go, lay down your tools
and tremors, where the hands do not invade,
but instead bless a place where harm too often stayed.

EPILOGUE: THIS BIG FAKE WORLD

The object is to not simply exist in this world
of radio clocks and moon pies, where holidays
and lunch breaks bring the only relief from
the machine that is our mind humming inside
of its shell. Shouldn't we make a fire out of
everyday things, build something out of too many
nails and not wonder if we are right to build
without permission from the other dull furniture?
Out of this small plot we are given, small plot
of cement and electrified wires, small plot
of razors and outlandish liquor names,
let's make a nest, each of us, of our own pieces
of glass and weeds and names we have found.
Somewhere along the banks of this liquid world
let all of us hold close to the lost and the unclear,
and, in our own odd little way, find some refuge here.

from SHARKS IN THE RIVERS

SHARKS IN THE RIVERS

We'll say unbelievable things
to each other in the early morning—

our blue coming up from our roots,
our water rising in our extraordinary limbs.

All night I dreamt of bonfires and burn piles
and ghosts of men, and spirits
behind those birds of flame.

I cannot tell anymore when a door opens or closes,
I can only hear the frame saying, *Walk through.*

It is a short walkway—
into another bedroom.

Consider the handle. Consider the key.

I say to a friend, how scared I am of sharks.

How I thought I saw them in the creek
across from my street.

I once watched for them, holding a bundle
of rattlesnake grass in my hand,
shaking like a weak-leaf girl.

She sends me an article from a recent *National Geographic* that says,

*Sharks bite fewer people each year than
New Yorkers do, according to Health Department records.*

Then she sends me on my way. Into the City of Sharks.

Through another doorway, I walk to the East River saying,

Sharks are people too.
Sharks are people too.
Sharks are people too.

I write all the things I need on the bottom
of my tennis shoes. I say, *Let's walk together.*

The sun behind me is like a fire.
Tiny flames in the river's ripples.

I say something to God, but he's not a living thing,
so I say it to the river, I say,

I want to walk through this doorway
but without all those ghosts on the edge,
I want them to stay here.
I want them to go on without me.

I want them to burn in the water.

FLOOD COMING

The pulled-apart world scatters
its bad news like a brush fire,
the ink bleeds out the day's undoing
and here we are again: alive.

The tributary of this riverine dark
widens into the mind's brief break.
Let the flood come, the rowdy water
beasts are knocking now and now.

What's left of the woods is closing in.
Don't run. Open your mouth big
to the rising and hope to your god
your good heart knows how to swim.

DIAGNOSIS: EVEN THE STILLAGUAMISH RIVER CANNOT STOP TIME

Your cat has dragged a dead bird onto the porch again.
Fragments of its dull wings still hang in the air, the real live
wind brings a cold rain up from the Sound. Your hands
are wet; time moves too fast. Things were easier earlier,
when the Snow Goose was open for business and the sun
lay its original light all up and down the Stillaguamish River.
Everything, now, is an interrogation. *Why this bird? Why
this interruption, soaked to the bone?* The river is still there—
steady and cunning with current. It does not answer,
but it loves the conversation; it is both the cat and the bird.
It is at once your body dissolved in this rain and your
beautiful wet hands trying to hold onto water.

OVERJOYED

What's the drunk waxwing supposed to do
when all day's been an orgy of red buds
on the winery's archway off Gehricke Road
and it's too far to make it home, too long
to fly, even as the sober crow goes. What's
the point of passion when the pyracantha
berries keep the blood turned toward
obsess, obsess. Don't you know those birds
are going to toss themselves to the streets
for some minor song of happiness? And
who can blame them? This life is hard.
And let me be the first to admit, when I
come across some jewel of pleasure, I too want
to squeeze that thing until even its seedy heart
evaporates like ethanol, want to throw my
bird-bones into the brush-fire until,
half-blind, all I can hear is the sound
of wings in the relentlessly delighted air.

CRUSH

Maybe my limbs are made
mostly for decoration—
the way I feel about
persimmons. You can't
really eat them. Or you
wouldn't want to. If you grab
the soft skin with your fist
it somehow feels funny,
like you've been here
before, and uncomfortable
too, like you'd rather
squish it between your teeth
impatiently, before spitting
the soft parts back up
to linger on the tongue
like burnt sugar or guilt.
For starters, it was all
an accident; you cut
the right branch
and a sort of light
woke up underneath,
and the inedible fruit
grew dark and needy.
Think crucial hanging.
Think crayon orange.
There is one low, leaning
heart-shaped globe left
and dearest, can you
tell, I am trying
to love you less.

THE NEW WORLD OF BEAUTY

Beauty in its optimal world,
denies all its adversaries,
>	says, *Boo*, says, *Who's there?*

>	And the ugly parts scatter.

When I met you, you had a boxer's body
>	and a mug to match your bruises.

You complained about the heat,
>	the small rooms, so stifling.

Gringo, with your hat to block out the world,
>	come a little closer.

There's a lion in a cage,
>	a lion in infinity (in here), pressed up against the bars.

It's got it worse than you.

>	Don't think about Laika in orbit.
>	Don't think about cringe and catastrophe.

There's a lion in a cage
>	just outside of Ensenada. Poor yellow beast,
in the desert of Cataviña.

His heart has been lost and
>	already prepared for dust.

>	Say something pretty about it. I dare you.

Something pretty. (Break it.)
Something pretty. (Kill it.)

Beauty will come to you, lie down at your feet,
    put its wild hair in your lap.

Will you know it, Gringo?

THE RUSSIAN RIVER

In the 1973 Ford LTD, we took Highway 12
and headed toward the wide Russian River.
It was the summer of our final year of high school;
we were all so stoned that the world was perfectly defined
by goodness and realness and the opposite of those.
It was 98 degrees and even with the windows open
it was hard to breathe. Outside of Guerneville
we found the party—beautiful bodies jumping off
the cliffs into the deepest part, a raft of natural
naked women floating like an old cigarette ad
down the current. I was going to marry you.
Hours into the afternoon we swam to each other
and walked upriver. I remember thinking this
was what life was, and what I had always wanted:
being pressed on a warm, flat rock, our wet imprint
there as if it would matter, *I am holding on. I am holding on.*

MARKETING LIFE FOR THOSE OF US LEFT

For Jessica Yen

Stuck in the answer of day,
all we've got are these people to rely on—
and trees, and the grasp of a river in the mind.

High hillside of home,
I'm waving from the cement center, can you see me?

All the beautiful girls in the office are laughing and I laugh
along. And all of us good people, honest and clean,

and what puts the mean in some of us?

Sumptuous mountain, midnight milkweed,
come to the valley of neon and no-crying.

I've got this big city in me. Pretty on fire, pretty high-wired.

It's been a year since Jess died; she said,
I always knew it would come down to pills in the applesauce.

And the house is not haunted, nor the office.

I wish they were, don't you?

We were wilder before—see-through shirts
and model boys and bouncers in hotel lobbies
across the country.

Who knew it would be hard to live to thirty-two?

A friend says the best way to love the world is to think of leaving.

We're all in trouble, you know?
Piles of empty stars we've tossed aside for the immediate kiss.

Push me around a bit, shake my pockets, I store everything
in my mouth. I'm going to make an apple out of plastic,
going to make a real star out of the apple, then
I'm going to sell it to you.

I'm going to tell you it's the most important thing.

I'm going to tell you I'm sorry, I'm going to crash
on your communal couch of unwanted.

Let's say bloom.
Let's say we're a miracle of technology.
It's harder not to say anything.

It's all we've got, say it, pinch me.
You're here. So am I. So there.

HARDWORKING AGREEMENT WITH A WEDNESDAY

I have an agreement with the day:
I won't talk too much.

I won't be the most complicated minute in its
configuration of hours.

Come to the office with me. Stay awhile.

The woman in the elevator (who's in sales) is so nice,
but she says my name over, and over, and over.

(Even when I don't say hers.)

She says, *Good morning, Ada.*
How was your evening, Ada?
Have a good day, Ada.

So my name becomes an advertisement, or a product
to be bought and sold. I want to take it back from her mouth.

I cannot stop looking at the bird out the window.

We've named him Stanley. He's half-angry,
half-slow, half-bird. One-and-a-half figurine.

I want him to live somewhere else, but it's not my decision.

He likes the rooftop of the high-rise,
the hot soft tar grasped in his claws. He likes the danger.
He likes the dirt on his beak. He likes it rough.

I want his flight to be my own,
as if wings themselves could be willed.

Let's fly south to Monterey, to water, to ether, to air.

Everything is off-limits.
Everything is unreal.
Everything is lament and let go.

Dear Today,
I have said too much, yet give me this—
I want to be a physical doll, just for now,
a stupid, splendid thing,
tumbled into the touchable day.

HOMESICK

In the Glen Ellen night, banned to the backyard
for running in the house, I and a particular tree
became fast friends in the green sequined summer.
I situated myself inside it, where I watched
the yellow of our kitchen window—my
soundproof family. I liked the shadows cast
in gobo-leaf prints on my bare limbs. I imagined
myself growing green sprouts and maroon bark
that shot into the dirt. Today in this terrible
cement city, I will do this bidding, but I tell you:
I am there, across from Sonoma Creek, still hidden
in the tree, where I cannot be unbelieved.

WAYS TO EASE YOUR ANIMAL MIND

A cloud of cormorants comes
flooding out of rushed wind,
out of sunned sea-bound waves.

The air is unwound with bird
and you are not lost in the least,
but a deliberate deserter.

Let go the oxcart.
Let go the claw and climb.

This fevered mess of world
is well-done. Lean in and nuzzle
its exceptional need to be yours.

THE CROSSING

For Cynthia

We drive up to Smokey Point
    and the Snoqualmie River is muddy.
The fish have been crossing for days—
    all night, the news of coho
crossings—sightings of those swimming
    beaming finners.

One band of sun holds its hands
    down on the field, but the water's still deep—
the inaccessible earth, the dark birds
    in scissors cut the sky
into gray and grayer, two halves
    of the same strange atmosphere.

The trees stand up straight for now and
    the old barbecue is gone, but a whole cement
village has bricked the land over in its place.
    Every neon sign says, *Stop.*
Every market sells a season
    (poor black-capped chickadee trapped in its rafters).

The medication has made your face different,
    your skin's not the same you've lived in,
we wait at the train tracks as a new
    deluge comes, a bold blundering sky of fresh
water. (A single leaf on a tree,
    one bigleaf maple-child, a wet dog on a cement heap.)

You say you wish there was a way
>   you could come back—
to find out who your wild son grows up to be,
>   if the house stands up to the years of rain,
if your dear husband stands up to the years of rain.
>   (A car alarm, a fire truck.)

Maybe there is a way—
>   like fish in the cold fall storms,
maybe we do, our bodies unskinned
>   and unadorned, making our way
to the place our beating belongs,
>   our pulsing light flashing up a river.

Silvery across a flooded highway,
>   our human faults forgiven, a returning to
the first uncomplicated river system,
>   blood to blood to blood, until we are carried
around in the world like one grateful fish
>   escaping the lure and seeing the same moon

it has seen for ten thousand years,
>   the same moon our other dear fishes see,
maybe, I say (my own tenuous connection),
>   maybe, (the railroad crossing released, the car
pushing toward home). *Maybe*, I say to you,
>   *Maybe we do come back.*

THE SAME THING

There's an awful story in the news.
For days you cannot sleep; it's too hot, it's too cold.

It's just a story in the news.

Not another human, not a whole country,
not another animal, just a piece of paper.

Then you feel a little better.
You go to the train and wear your headphones,
you listen to a sad song that sounds familiar.

You pass a store window and there's someone
you don't know walking where you're walking: heels,
a summer dress, hair tied up too fancy for the week.

The television says tomorrow night they will
shed some light on hell.

How far do we need to search for some bad thing?
Hell is not beneath us, not a bargaining chip with your children.

You come home on the train and you have
bought gifts and tried to be decent.

This is how your life will go, you know that. Day after day.

Awful acceptance: the soft life of your footprints.

You start to think of the alternative,
you shake your real shirt off in the hallway.

Would it be the same if you were born in Mexico? Life.
        Cuba? Ireland? 1974?

You miss everyone. Even the people you read about today
you didn't know, their faces on the brain as if on paper.

You sit on the balcony,
which is really a fire escape, but you call it
the balcony to make it sound better.
You wear the slip your grandmother gave you

fifteen years ago, the weather is nice, California nice.

You sing a little, call your family, you think, *things aren't so bad.*

You say you love the world, so love the world.

Maybe you don't even say it for yourself,
maybe you move your mouth like everyone
moves their mouth. Maybe your mouth is the same
mouth as everyone's, all trying to say the same thing.

BIRD BOUND FOR A GOOD WORLD

In the car ride to the Cape we wrought ourselves
    a radio show. My job was to keep repeating, in the voice
of a circus announcer, *Cape Cod National Seashore, step right up.*

Abraham had the job of quiet Wisconsin banter about the birds
we were bound to see now that our walls had forgiven us this.

We began a list, the easiest first:

    black-backed gull, piping plover,

We said we were the long-suffering kettle pond.
We said we were the orphans of pavement.

    cormorants, common terns, mergansers,

We said we'd like to drink whiskey when we got there.
We said, finally, we didn't love anyone and it felt wonderful.

    eiders, egrets, great blue herons,

I said I loved rocks and water and fish.
Abraham said he loved the birch woods and leaves.

    chickadees with their caps, dear, dear, sweet swallows.

We come so far from our homes,
my valley of the moon,
his Ladysmith of the woods.

And here we are, diligent birds,
trying to make a small life out of paper and string.

    Seed-hoarder, stream-nester,
warm-blooded, beak-lover, bird-speaker—

go to the water, bird,
love the blue world, bird,
money means nothing, bird,
clothes mean nothing, bird,
keep going into the world, bird,
startle the sad spring air with the whirring of your wings.

DROWNING IN PARADISE

The low-hanging hibiscus coos out
its swollen-mouth flower song
to the rare bee holding its tongue
and I'm drunk on the bully world again—
a fueled up fluster coming on.
Look, even two oceans can collide
here in the bellies of white islands.
Splurge and risk in the conch-dark
night—I'm going to walk into the water's
frothy rim. Come here shark. Come
here barracuda. Love the sweet artifacts
of this body. Carry me in the world-class
rattle of a wave. I want the big bite, one
restless, tooth-filled mouth to take me down.

TO THE BUSTED AMONG US

But everyone is busted a little.

No consciousness of the breaking, just the history
of a dirty footprint—even the easy stuff,
the small conversations about our worth.

(To be an anonymous object,
the innocuous heart, the smallest part of flesh.)

On Withers Avenue, a rat circled the bottom of a trash can,
threw itself against the plastic green walls of its new world.
I heard it. I removed the top. I put the top back on.

(Small brilliant hole in the dark, let me out.)

Standing in my ridiculous human clothes,
I argued with the rat. I asked him,

Are you rabid?
Are you crazy?
Are you responsible for the plague?

He didn't answer; he threw himself again.

Are you mean?
Did you hurt your children?
Did you hurt anyone?

I want to tell you that I let that rat out,

that kindness overwhelmed the tough pout of people-cleanliness.
I want to tell you I put him in a shoe box
and brought him to the country, fed him corn and taught him to read.

(Un-gettable parallel time, fathomless choices.)

I say to a stranger, *I am harmless.*

But the word doesn't seem right. I have been harmed,
but I do not wish to do harm, but I could do harm.
(I am not without desire.)

I want to tell you the rat moved in with me, we made a good living.

But, I tell you, I let him be.

I think he might have managed to release himself,
he was not harmless. He had intent. Flirting with the world.

He'll show up one day, long-wandered in the weather.

He just needed someone subversive to bend in
real close and say,

You can rustle all you want,
you can reinvent the shout,
but you got your rat-self in there,
now, get your cunning rat-self out.

from BRIGHT DEAD THINGS

HOW TO TRIUMPH LIKE A GIRL

I like the lady horses best,
how they make it all look easy,
like running 40 miles per hour
is as fun as taking a nap, or grass.
I like their lady horse swagger,
after winning. Ears up, girls, ears up!
But mainly, let's be honest, I like
that they're ladies. As if this big
dangerous animal is also a part of me,
that somewhere inside the delicate
skin of my body, there pumps
an 8-pound female horse heart,
giant with power, heavy with blood.
Don't you want to believe it?
Don't you want to lift my shirt and see
the huge beating genius machine
that thinks, no, it knows,
it's going to come in first.

DURING THE IMPOSSIBLE AGE OF EVERYONE

1.

There are so many people who've come before us,
arrows and wagon wheels, obsidian tools, buffalo.
Look out at the meadow, you can almost see them,
generations dissolved in the bluegrass and hay.
I want to try and be terrific. Even for an hour.

2.

If you walk long enough, your crowded head clears,
like how all the cattle run off loudly as you approach.
This fence is a good fence, but I doubt my own haywire
will hold up to all this blank sky, so open and explicit.
I'm like a fence, or a cow, or that word, *yonder*.

3.

There is a slow tractor traffic hollering outside,
and I'd like not to be traffic, but the window shaking.
Your shoes are piled up with mine, and the heat
comes on, makes a simple noise, a dog-yawn.
People have done this before, but not us.

THE LAST MOVE

It was only months when it felt like I had been
washing the dishes forever.

Hardwood planks under the feet, a cord to the sky.
What is it to go to a *We* from an *I*?

Each time he left for an errand, the walls
would squeeze me in. I cried over the nonexistent bathmat, wet
    floor of him,
how south we were, far away in the outskirts.

(All the new bugs.)

I put my apron on as a joke and waltzed around carrying
a zucchini like a child.

This is Kentucky, not New York, and I am not important.

This was before we got the dog even, and before I trusted
the paralyzing tranquilizer of love stuck
in the flesh of my neck.

Back home, in my apartment, another woman lived there.
In Brooklyn, by the deli, where everything
was clean and contained.

(Where I grieved my deaths.)

I took to my hands and knees. I was thinking about the novel
I was writing. The great heavy chest of live animals
I had been dragging around for years; what's life?

I made the house so clean (shine and shine and shine).

I was suspicious of the monkey sounds of Kentucky's birds,
judging crackles, rusty mailbox, spiders in the magnolia tree,
tornado talk, dead June bugs like pinto beans.

Somewhere I had heard that, after noting the lack
of water pressure in an old hotel in Los Angeles,
they found a woman's body at the bottom
of the cistern.

Imagine, just thinking the water was low, just wanting
to take a shower.

After that, when the water would act weird,
spurt, or gurgle, I'd imagine a body, a woman, a me
just years ago, freely single, happily unaccounted for,
at the lowest curve of the water tower.

Yes, and over and over,
I'd press her limbs down with a long pole
until she was still.

HOW FAR AWAY WE ARE

So we might understand each other better:
I'm leaning on the cracked white window ledge
in my nice pink slippers lined with fake pink fur.
The air conditioning is sensational. Outside,
we've put up a cheap picnic table beneath the maple
but the sun's too hot to sit in, so the table glows
on alone like bleached-out bones in the heat.
Yesterday, so many dead in Norway. Today,
a big-voiced singer found dead in her London flat.
And this country's gone standstill and criminal.
I want to give you something, or I want to take
something from you. But I want to feel the exchange,
the warm hand on the shoulder, the song coming out
and the ear holding on to it. Maybe we could meet
at that table under the tree, just right out there.
I'm passing the idea to you in this note:
the table, the tree, the pure heat of late July.
We could be in that same safe place watching
the sugar maple throw down its winged seeds
like the tree wants to give us something too—
some sweet goodness that's so hard to take.

THE QUIET MACHINE

I'm learning so many different ways to be quiet. There's how I stand in the lawn, that's one way. There's also how I stand in the field across from the street, that's another way because I'm farther from people and therefore more likely to be alone. There's how I don't answer the phone, and how I sometimes like to lie down on the floor in the kitchen and pretend I'm not home when people knock. There's daytime silent when I stare, and a nighttime silent when I do things. There's shower silent and bath silent and California silent and Kentucky silent and car silent and then there's the silence that comes back, a million times bigger than me, sneaks into my bones and wails and wails and wails until I can't be quiet anymore. That's how this machine works.

I REMEMBER THE CARROTS

I haven't given up on trying to live a good life,
a really good one even, sitting in the kitchen
in Kentucky, imagining how agreeable I'll be—
the advance of fulfillment, and of desire—
all these needs met, then unmet again.
When I was a kid, I was excited about carrots,
their spidery neon tops in the garden's plot.
And so I ripped them all out. I broke the new roots
and carried them, like a prize, to my father
who scolded me, rightly, for killing his whole crop.
I loved them: my own bright dead things.
I'm thirty-five and remember all that I've done wrong.
Yesterday I was nice, but in truth I resented
the contentment of the field. Why must we practice
this surrender? What I mean is: there are days
I still want to kill the carrots because I can.

SOMEPLACE LIKE MONTANA

For Trish

Now when I go to the grocery store,
I'm amazed at the wide aisles of bright
food and food-stuffs, and it's nothing like
the bodega I shopped in for years,
in Brooklyn, between the bars we liked.
Once, when I was going for groceries,
I ran into T, and we decided we needed
to drink rather than shop, and we did.

There were a lot of beers on tap,
and the taps were all different like toys
in a dentist's toy chest, so I said,
I'll have what she's having,
and maybe it was snowing out,
and it seemed to be at a time when
every shirt I bought at the secondhand store
would turn out to be see-through,
but I wouldn't know it until I was out.
So, a lot of conversations would start,
Is this shirt see-through? And it was.

We talked for a long time, grocery bags
empty on the chair, and we both talked about
moving to someplace like Montana
and how sometimes it would be nice
to see more sky than just this little square
between the bridges and buildings,
but then we'd miss Brooklyn, and each other,
and we ordered another beer.

T was writing a play, also some articles,
and we both just needed some money,
and maybe to make out with someone
who wasn't an asshole. But also, we wanted
to make great art. T was really good at naming
things so we decided she should be a *Titleologist*
and she liked that, so she agreed.

*What would we do if we lived in
someplace like Montana?*

*We'd go for walks, and look at trees,
and write and look at the sky.*

*Yes, and we'd cook and go to those huge grocery stores
that have toy cars attached to the carts so kids
can pretend to be driving.*

Yes, and we'd probably have kids, too.

All of this seemed really far off and not like us at all,
so we ordered another beer and said, *Life is long.*

Now, I'm walking around the grocery store
in Kentucky and I've just looked at trees, and sky,
and I should write something, so I ask T to tell me
what to write about, she says, *Saturation*, and I think
of that feeling when you're really full, or life is full
and you can't think of anything else that could fit in it,
but then even more sky comes and more days
and there is so much to remember and swallow.
I ask T what I should call the thing I write about
Saturation, because she's a titleologist, and she says,
Someplace Like Montana.

STATE BIRD

Confession: I did not want to live here,
not among the goldenrod, wild onions,
or the dropseed, not waist-high in the barrel-
aged brown corn water, not with the million-
dollar racehorses, nor the tightly wound
round hay bales. Not even in the old tobacco
weigh station we live in, with its heavy metal
safe doors that frame our bricked bedroom
like the mouth of a strange beast yawning
to suck us in, each night, like air. I denied it,
this new land. But love, I'll concede this:
whatever state you are, I'll be that state's bird,
the loud, obvious blur of song people point to
when they wonder where it is you've gone.

DOWNHEARTED

Six horses died in a tractor-trailer fire.
There. That's the hard part. I wanted
to tell you straight away so we could
grieve together. So many sad things,
that's just one on a long recent list
that loops and elongates in the chest,
in the diaphragm, in the alveoli. What
is it they say, *heartsick* or *downhearted*?
I picture a heart lying down on the floor
of the torso, pulling up the blankets
over its head, thinking this pain will
go on forever (even though it won't).
The heart is watching Lifetime movies
and wishing, and missing all the good
parts of her that she has forgotten.
The heart is so tired of beating
herself up, she wants to stop it still,
but also she wants the blood to return,
wants to bring in the thrill and wind of the ride,
the fast pull of life driving underneath her.
What the heart wants? The heart wants
her horses back.

WHAT IT LOOKS LIKE TO US
AND THE WORDS WE USE

All these great barns out here in the outskirts,
black creosote boards knee-deep in the bluegrass.
They look so artfully abandoned, even in use.
You say they look like arks after the sea's
dried up, I say they look like pirate ships,
and I think of that walk in my valley where
J said, *You don't believe in God?* And I said,
*No. I believe in this connection we all have
to nature, to each other, to the universe.*
And she said, *Yeah, God.* And how we stood there,
low beasts among the white oaks, Spanish moss,
and spider webs, obsidian shards stuck in our pockets,
woodpecker flurry, and I refused to call it so.
So instead, we looked up at the unruly sky,
its clouds in simple animal shapes we could name
though we knew they were really just clouds—
disorderly, and marvelous, and ours.

COWER

I'm cold in my heart, coal-hard
knot in the mountain buried
deep in the boarded-up mine. So,
I let death in, learn to prospect
the between-dreams of the dying,
the one dream that tells you when
to throw up, the other, when
you're in pain. I tell you
I will love someone that you
will never meet, death's warm
breath at the mouth
of the body's holler.
You are crying in the shower.
I am crying near the shower.
Your body a welcomed-red
fire-starter in steam and I think,
How scared I would be
if I were death. How could I
come to this house, come
to this loved being, see
the mountain's power
and dare blast you down.
I dry you off and think,
if I were death come to take you,
your real-earth explosives,
I would be terrified.

RELENTLESS

Sun in the cool expressway underpass air
and Ma calls, says it's nice out today
during her long walk through the vineyard
where spring's pushed out every tizzy-tongued
flower known to the valley's bosom of light.
I say, *Look, we're talking about the weather,*
and she says, *You know, it does help you
see the person you're talking to.* (The difference
in a wind-blown winter's walk in January cold
and the loose steps of sun on far-off shoulders.)
Then I say, *Now, we're talking about talking
about the weather. It's very meta of us.*
Yes, she says, *we could go on like this forever.*
And it's been exactly two months since
C died, my hands holding her head, odd
extraordinary February sun gone down
on the smooth slope of green grass, and
all my father and I had done all day was
talk about two things: the weather and her
breathing. (That machine-body gone harsh
in its prolonging and the loud gasping sigh of dying,
thick as a hawk's cry, breaking out in the cloudless
atmosphere.) Some impossibly still moment,
we stood looking at the long field's pull
and we wanted her to die, for her sake,
wanted the motor of body to give up and go.
How strange this silent longing for death,
as if you could make the sun not come up,
the world's wheeling and wheeling its seasons
like a cruel continuation of stubborn force.
But that's not how it happens. Instead, light

escapes from the heart's room and for a moment
you believe the clock will stop itself. Absence.
You see: light escapes from a body at night
and in the morning, despite the oppressive vacancy
of her leaving's shadow, light comes up
over the mountains and it is and it is and it is.

THE RIVETER

What I didn't say
when she asked me
why I knew so much
about dying was that,
for me, it was work.
When Dad called to say
we had a month, I made a list.
I called in my team
to my office in a high rise,
those Rosies of know-how,
those that had lost someone loved,
those that had done the assembly line
of a home death, and said,
*What's this about not keeping
her on TPN?* One woman,
who was still soft with sadness,
said, *It depends on whether
she wants to die of heart failure
or to drown in her own fluids.*
I nodded, and wrote that down
like this was a meeting
about a client who wasn't happy.
What about hospice? I asked.
They said, *They'll help,
but your dad and you guys
will do most of it.*
I put a star by that.
We had a plan of action.
When this happens, we do this.
When that happens, we do that.
But what I forgot
was that it was our plan,

not hers, not the one doing the dying,
this was a plan for those
who still had a *next*.
See, our job was simple:
keep on living. Her job was harder,
the hardest. Her job,
her work, was to let the machine
of survival break down,
make the factory fail,
to know that this war was winless,
to know that she would singlehandedly
destroy us all.

AFTER YOU TOSS AROUND THE ASHES

When she was dying, it was impossible to see forward to the next minute. What was happening—for whole weeks—was all that was happening and happening and happening. Months before that, I got the dumb soup wrong. How awful. It was all she wanted and I had gotten it wrong. Then, in the airless days when it was really happening, we started to power panic that we didn't know enough. What should we do with her ashes? *Water or dirt. Water or dirt.* Once, she asked to just be thrown into the river where we used to go, still alive, but not living anymore. After it was done, I couldn't go back to my life. You understand, right? It wasn't the same. I couldn't tell if I loved myself more or less. It wasn't until later, when I moved in with him and stood outside on our patchy imperfect lawn, that I remembered what had been circling in me: I am beautiful. I am full of love. I am dying.

TORN

Witness the wet dead snake,
its long hexagonal pattern weaved
around its body like a code for creation,
curled up cold on the newly tarred road.
Let us begin with the snake: the fact
of death, the poverty of place, of skin
and surface. See how the snake is cut
in two—its body divided from its brain.
Imagine now, how it moves still, both
sides, the tail dancing, the head dancing.
Believe it is the mother and the father.
Believe it is the mouth and the words.
Believe it is the sin and the sinner—
the tempting, the taking, the apple, the fall,
every one of us guilty, the story of us all.
But then return to the snake, pitiful dead
thing, forcefully denying the split of its being,
longing for life back as a whole, wanting
you to see it for what it is: something
that loves itself so much it moves across
the boundaries of death to touch itself
once more, to praise both divided sides
equally, as if it was easy.

ADAPTATION

It was, for a time, a loud twittering flight
of psychedelic-colored canaries: a cloud
of startle and get-out in the ornamental
irons of the rib cage. Nights when the moon
was wide like the great eye of a universal
beast coming close for a kill, it was a cave
of bitten bones and snake skins, eggshell dust,
and charred scraps of a frozen-over flame.
All the things it has been: kitchen knife
and the ancient carp's frown, cavern of rust
and worms in the airless tire swing,
cactus barb, cut-down tree, dead cat
in the plastic crate. Still, how the great middle
ticker marched on, and from all its four chambers
to all its forgiveness, unlocked the sternum's
door, reversed and reshaped until it was a new
bright carnal species, more accustomed to grief,
and ecstatic at the sight of you.

THE CONDITIONAL

Say tomorrow doesn't come.
Say the moon becomes an icy pit.
Say the sweet-gum tree is petrified.
Say the sun's a foul black tire fire.
Say the owl's eyes are pinpricks.
Say the raccoon's a hot tar stain.
Say the shirt's plastic ditch-litter.
Say the kitchen's a cow's corpse.
Say we never get to see it: bright
future, stuck like a bum star, never
coming close, never dazzling.
Say we never meet her. Never him.
Say we spend our last moments staring
at each other, hands knotted together,
clutching the dog, watching the sky burn.
Say, *It doesn't matter.* Say, *That would be
enough.* Say you'd still want this: us alive,
right here, feeling lucky.

from THE CARRYING

ANCESTORS

I've come here from the rocks, the bone-like chert,
    obsidian, lava rock. I've come here from the trees—

chestnut, bay laurel, toyon, acacia, redwood, cedar,

one thousand oaks
    that bend with moss and old-man's beard.
I was born on a green couch on Carriger Road between
    the vineyards and the horse pasture.

I don't remember what I first saw, the brick of light
    that unhinged me from the beginning. I don't remember

my brother's face, my mother, my father.

    Later, I remember leaves, through car windows,
through bedroom windows, through the classroom window,

the way they shaded and patterned the ground, all that
    power from roots. Imagine you must survive

without running? I've come from the lacing patterns of leaves,

    I do not know where else I belong.

THE LEASH

After the birthing of bombs of forks and fear,
the frantic automatic weapons unleashed,
the spray of bullets into a crowd holding hands,
that brute sky opening in a slate-metal maw
that swallows only the unsayable in each of us, what's
left? Even the hidden nowhere river is poisoned
orange and acidic by a coal mine. How can
you not fear humanity, want to lick the creek
bottom dry, to suck the deadly water up into
your own lungs, like venom? Reader, I want to
say: *Don't die.* Even when silvery fish after fish
comes back belly up, and the country plummets
into a crepitating crater of hatred, isn't there still
something singing? The truth is: I don't know.
But sometimes I swear I hear it, the wound closing
like a rusted-over garage door, and I can still move
my living limbs into the world without too much
pain, can still marvel at how the dog runs straight
toward the pickup trucks breaknecking down
the road, because she thinks she loves them,
because she's sure, without a doubt, that the loud
roaring things will love her back, her soft small self
alive with desire to share her goddamn enthusiasm,
until I yank the leash back to save her because
I want her to survive forever. *Don't die*, I say,
and we decide to walk for a bit longer, starlings
high and fevered above us, winter coming to lay
her cold corpse down upon this little plot of earth.
Perhaps we are always hurtling our bodies toward
the thing that will obliterate us, begging for love
from the speeding passage of time, and so maybe,
like the dog obedient at my heels, we can walk together
peacefully, at least until the next truck comes.

THE RAINCOAT

When the doctor suggested surgery
and a brace for all my youngest years,
my parents scrambled to take me
to massage therapy, deep tissue work,
osteopathy, and soon my crooked spine
unspooled a bit, I could breathe again,
and move more in a body unclouded
by pain. My mom would tell me to sing
songs to her the whole forty-five-minute
drive to Middle Two Rock Road and forty-
five minutes back from physical therapy.
She'd say that even my voice sounded unfettered
by my spine afterward. So I sang and sang,
because I thought she liked it. I never
asked her what she gave up to drive me,
or how her day was before this chore. Today,
at her age, I was driving myself home from yet
another spine appointment, singing along
to some maudlin but solid song on the radio,
and I saw a mom take her raincoat off
and give it to her young daughter when
a storm took over the afternoon. My god,
I thought, my whole life I've been under her
raincoat thinking it was somehow a marvel
that I never got wet.

THE VULTURE & THE BODY

On my way to the fertility clinic,
        I pass five dead animals.

First a raccoon with all four paws to the sky
        like he's going to catch whatever bullshit load
falls on him next.

Then, a grown coyote, his golden furred body soft against the white
        cement lip of the traffic barrier. Trickster no longer,
an eye closed to what's coming.

Close to the water tower that says "Florence, Y'all," which means
I'm near Cincinnati, but still in the bluegrass state,
        and close to my exit, I see

three dead deer, all staggered but together, and I realize as I speed
past in my death machine that they are a family. I say something

to myself that's between a prayer and a curse—how dare we live
        on this earth.

I want to tell my doctor about how we all hold a duality
        in our minds: futures entirely different, footloose or forged.

I want to tell him how lately, it's enough to be reminded that my
body is not just my body, but that I'm made of old stars and so's he,
        and that last Tuesday,

I sat alone in the car by the post office and just *was*
        for a whole hour, no one knowing how to find me, until
I got out, the sound of the car door shutting like a gun,

and mailed letters, all of them saying, *Thank you.*

But in the clinic, the sonogram wand showing my follicles, he asks
if I have any questions, and says, *Things are getting exciting.*

I want to say, *But what about all the dead animals?*

But he goes quicksilver, and I'm left to pull my panties up like a big girl.

Some days there is a violent sister inside of me, and a red ladder
    that wants to go elsewhere.

I drive home on the other side of the road, going south now.
The white coat has said I'm ready, and I watch as a vulture
    crosses over me, heading toward

the carcasses I haven't properly mourned or even forgiven.
    What if, instead of carrying

  a child, I am supposed to carry grief?

The great black scavenger flies parallel now, each of us speeding,
intently and driven, toward what we've been taught to do with death.

DANDELION INSOMNIA

The big-ass bees are back, tipsy, sun drunk
and heavy with thick knitted leg warmers
of pollen. I was up all night again so today's
yellow hours seem strange and hallucinogenic.
The neighborhood is lousy with mowers, crazy
dogs, and people mending what winter ruined.
What I can't get over is something simple, easy:
How could a dandelion seed head seemingly
grow overnight? A neighbor mows the lawn
and bam, the next morning, there's a hundred
dandelion seed heads straight as arrows
and proud as cats high above any green blade
of manicured grass. It must bug some folks,
a flower so tricky it can reproduce asexually,
making perfect identical selves, bam, another me,
bam, another me. I can't help it—I root
for that persecuted rosette so hyper in its
own making it seems to devour the land.
Even its name, translated from the French
dent de lion, means lion's tooth. It's vicious,
made for a time that requires tenacity, a way
of remaking the toughest self while everyone
else is asleep.

DEAD STARS

Out here, there's a bowing even the trees are doing.
    Winter's icy hand at the back of all of us.
Black bark, slick yellow leaves, a kind of stillness that feels
so mute it's almost in another year.

I am a hearth of spiders these days: a nest of trying.

We point out the stars that make Orion as we take out
    the trash, the rolling containers a song of suburban thunder.

It's almost romantic as we adjust the waxy blue
    recycling bin until you say, *Man, we should really learn
some new constellations.*

And it's true. We keep forgetting about Antlia, Centaurus,
    Draco, Lacerta, Hydra, Lyra, Lynx.

But mostly we're forgetting we're dead stars too, my mouth is full
    of dust and I wish to reclaim the rising—

to lean in the spotlight of streetlight with you, toward
    what's larger within us, toward how we were born.

Look, we are not unspectacular things.
    We've come this far, survived this much. What

would happen if we decided to survive more? To love harder?

What if we stood up with our synapses and flesh and said, *No.
    No*, to the rising tides.

Stood for the many mute mouths of the sea, of the land?

What would happen if we used our bodies to bargain

for the safety of others, for earth,
 if we declared a clean night, if we stopped being terrified,

if we launched our demands into the sky, made ourselves so big
people could point to us with the arrows they make in their minds,

rolling their trash bins out, after all of this is over?

WHAT I WANT TO REMEMBER

Right before General Vallejo's home,
with its stately stone and yellow walls,

there's a field along the footpath
where spring rains bring the frogs,

a whole symphony of them, breaking
open the hours just after the sun

sinks into the Pacific Ocean only
an hour away. Why am I placing

you here? I'm on a plane going west
and all the humans are so loud

it hurts the blood. But once I sat
next to a path that was still warm

from the day's heat, cross-legged
with my friend named Echo who taught

me how to amplify the strange sound
the frogs made by cupping my ears.

I need to hold this close within me,
when today's news is full of dead children,

their faces opening their mouths for air
that will not come. Once I was a child too

and my friend and I sat for maybe an hour,
eyes adjusting to the night sky, cupping

and uncupping our ears to hear
the song the tenderest animals made.

OVERPASS

The road wasn't as hazardous then,
when I'd walk to the steel guardrail,
lean my bendy girl body over, and stare
at the cold creek water. In a wet spring,
the water'd run clear and high, minnows
mouthing the sand and silt, a crawdad
shadowed by the shore's long reeds.
I could stare for hours, something
always new in each watery wedge—
a bottle top, a man's black boot, a toad.
Once, a raccoon's carcass, half under
the overpass, half out, slowly decayed
over months. I'd check on him each day,
watching until the white bones of his hand
were totally skinless and seemed to reach
out toward the sun as it hit the water,
showing all five of his sweet tensile fingers
still clinging. I don't think I worshipped
him, his deadness, but I liked the evidence
of him, how it felt like a job to daily
take note of his shifting into the sand.

WONDER WOMAN

Standing at the swell of the muddy Mississippi
after the urgent care doctor had just said, *Well,
sometimes shit happens*, I fell fast and hard
for New Orleans all over again. Pain pills swirled
in the purse along with a spell for later. It's taken
a while for me to admit, I am in a raging battle
with my body, a spinal column thirty-five degrees
bent, vertigo that comes and goes like a DC Comics
villain nobody can kill. Invisible pain is both
a blessing and a curse. *You always look so happy*,
said a stranger once as I shifted to my good side
grinning. But that day, alone on the riverbank,
brass blaring from the Steamboat Natchez,
out of the corner of my eye, I saw a girl, maybe half my age,
dressed, for no apparent reason, as Wonder Woman.
She strutted by in all her strength and glory, invincible,
eternal, and when I stood to clap (because who wouldn't have),
she bowed and posed like she knew I needed a myth—
a woman, by a river, indestructible.

THE REAL REASON

I don't have any tattoos is not my story to tell. It's my
mother's. Once, walking down Bedford Avenue in my twenties,

I called her as I did, as I do. I told her how I wanted a tattoo
on the back of my neck. Something minor, but permanent,

and she is an artist, I wanted her to create the design, a symbol,
a fish I dream of every night. An underwater talisman, a mother's

gift on my body. To be clear, I thought she'd be honored. But do we
ever really know each other fully? A silence like a hospital room; she

was in tears. I swore then that I wouldn't get one. Wouldn't let a needle
touch my neck, my arm, my torso. I'd stay me, my skin the skin

she welcomed me into the world with. It wasn't until later that
I knew it wasn't so much the tattoo, but the marking, the idea

of scars. What you don't know (and this is why this is not my story)
is that my mother is scarred from burns over a great deal of her body.

Most from an explosion that took her first child she was carrying
in her belly, others from the skin grafts where they took skin to cover

what needed it. She was in her late twenties when that happened.
Outside her studio in the center of town. You have to understand,

my mother is beautiful. Tall and elegant, thin and strong. I have not
known her any other way, her skin that I mapped with my young

fingers, its strange hardness in places, its patterns like quilts here,
riverbeds there. She's wondrous, preternatural, survived fire,

the ending of an unborn child. Heat and flame and death, all made
her into something seemingly magical, a phoenixess. What I know

now is she wanted something else for me. For me to wake each
morning and recognize my own flesh, for this one thing she made—

me—to remain how she intended, for one of us
to make it out unscathed.

THE YEAR OF THE GOLDFINCHES

There were two that hung and hovered
by the mud puddle and the musk thistle.
Flitting from one splintered fence post
to another, bathing in the rainwater's glint
like it was a mirror to some other universe
where things were more acceptable, easier
than the place I lived. I'd watch for them:
the bright peacocking male, the low-watt
female, on each morning walk, days spent
digging for some sort of elusive answer
to the question my curving figure made.
Later, I learned that they were a symbol
of resurrection. Of course they were,
my two yellow-winged twins feasting
on thorns and liking it.

SUNDOWN & ALL THE DAMAGE DONE

Nearly nine and still the sun's not slunk
into its nightly digs. The burnt-meat smell
of midweek cookouts and wet grass
hangs in the air like loose familiar summer
garb. Standing by the magnolia tree, I think
if I were to live as long as she did, I'd have
eleven more years. And if I were to live as long
as him, I'd have forty-nine. As long as him,
I'd be dead already. As long as her, this
would be my final year. There's a strange
contentment to this countdown, a nodding
to this time, where I get to stand under
the waxy leaves of the ancient genus, a tree
that appeared before even the bees, and
watch as fireflies land on the tough tepals
until each broad flower glows like a torchlit
mausoleum. They call the beetle's conspicuous
bioluminescence "a cold light," but why then
do I still feel so much fire?

A NEW NATIONAL ANTHEM

The truth is, I've never cared for the National
Anthem. If you think about it, it's not a good
song. Too high for most of us with "the rockets'
red glare" and then there are the bombs.
(Always, always there is war and bombs.)
Once, I sang it at homecoming and threw
even the tenacious high school band off key.
But the song didn't mean anything, just a call
to the field, something to get through before
the pummeling of youth. And what of the stanzas
we never sing, the third that mentions "no refuge
could save the hireling and the slave"? Perhaps
the truth is every song of this country
has an unsung third stanza, something brutal
snaking underneath us as we absentmindedly sing
the high notes with a beer sloshing in the stands
hoping our team wins. Don't get me wrong, I do
like the flag, how it undulates in the wind
like water, elemental, and best when it's humbled,
brought to its knees, clung to by someone who
has lost everything, when it's not a weapon,
when it flickers, when it folds up so perfectly
you can keep it until it's needed, until you can
love it again, until the song in your mouth feels
like sustenance, a song where the notes are sung
by even the ageless woods, the shortgrass plains,
the Red River Gorge, the fistful of land left
unpoisoned, that song that's our birthright,
that's sung in silence when it's too hard to go on,
that sounds like someone's rough fingers weaving

into another's, that sounds like a match being lit in an endless cave, the song that says my bones are your bones, and your bones are my bones, and isn't that enough?

THE CONTRACT SAYS: WE'D LIKE THE CONVERSATION TO BE BILINGUAL

When you come, bring your brown-
ness so we can be sure to please

the funders. Will you check this
box; we're applying for a grant.

Do you have any poems that speak
to troubled teens? Bilingual is best.

Would you like to come to dinner
with the patrons and sip Patrón?

Will you tell us the stories that make
us uncomfortable, but not complicit?

Don't read us the one where you
are just like us. Born to a green house,

garden, don't tell us how you picked
tomatoes and ate them in the dirt

watching vultures pick apart another
bird's bones in the road. Tell us the one

about your father stealing hubcaps
after a colleague said that's what his

kind did. Tell us how he came
to the meeting wearing a poncho

and tried to sell the man his hubcaps
back. Don't mention your father

was a teacher, spoke English, loved
making beer, loved baseball, tell us

again about the poncho, the hubcaps,
how he stole them, how he did the thing

he was trying to prove he didn't do.

INSTRUCTIONS ON NOT GIVING UP

More than the fuchsia funnels breaking out
of the crabapple tree, more than the neighbor's
almost obscene display of cherry limbs shoving
their cotton candy–colored blossoms to the slate
sky of spring rains, it's the greening of the trees
that really gets to me. When all the shock of white
and taffy, the world's baubles and trinkets, leave
the pavement strewn with the confetti of aftermath,
the leaves come. Patient, plodding, a green skin
growing over whatever winter did to us, a return
to the strange idea of continuous living despite
the mess of us, the hurt, the empty. Fine then,
I'll take it, the tree seems to say, a new slick leaf
unfurling like a fist to an open palm, I'll take it all.

CARRYING

The sky's white with November's teeth,
and the air is ash and woodsmoke.
A flush of color from the dying tree,
a cargo train speeding through, and there,
that's me, standing in the wintering
grass watching the dog suffer the cold
leaves. I'm not large from this distance,
just a fence post, a hedge of holly.
Wider still, beyond the rumble of overpass,
mares look for what's left of green
in the pasture, a few weanlings kick
out, and theirs is the same sky, white
like a calm flag of surrender pulled taut.
A few farms over, there's our mare,
her belly barrel-round with foal, or idea
of foal. It's Kentucky, late fall, and any
mare worth her salt is carrying the next
potential stakes winner. Ours, her coat
thicker with the season's muck, leans against
the black fence and this image is heavy
within me. How my own body, empty,
clean of secrets, knows how to carry her,
knows we were all meant for something.

WHAT I DIDN'T KNOW BEFORE

was how horses simply give birth to other
horses. Not a baby by any means, not
a creature of liminal spaces, but already
a four-legged beast hellbent on walking,
scrambling after the mother. A horse gives way
to another horse and then suddenly there are
two horses, just like that. That's how I loved you.
You, off the long train from Red Bank carrying
a coffee as big as your arm, a bag with two
computers swinging in it unwieldily at your
side. I remember we broke into laughter
when we saw each other. What was between
us wasn't a fragile thing to be coddled, cooed
over. It came out fully formed, ready to run.

LOVE POEM WITH APOLOGIES FOR MY APPEARANCE

Sometimes, I think you get the worst
of me. The much-loved loose forest-green
sweatpants, the long bra-less days, hair
knotted and uncivilized, a shadowed brow
where the devilish thoughts do their hoofed
dance on the brain. I'd like to say this means
I love you, the stained white cotton T-shirt,
the tears, pistachio shells, the mess of orange
peels on my desk, but it's different than that.
I move in this house with you, the way I move
in my mind, unencumbered by beauty's cage.
I do like I do in the tall grass, more animal-me
than much else. I'm wrong, it is that I love you,
but it's more that when you say it back, lights
out, a cold wind through curtains, for maybe
the first time in my life, I believe it.

LOSING

After your father gets lost for the third time,
    you get angry because he won't answer his phone.

Part of me wants him to stay lost. God, what has stolen my generosity?

He pours a bowl of cereal and milk and leaves the refrigerator door open.
    He calls you boss and me mother. *Yes, Mother*, he says and rolls

his eyes when I tell him to eat something, to clean up after himself.

Would I be more patient with a child? Would I love the smallness
    of a life more than the gone-ness of the mind? Yes.

I don't know what to do with him, so I cook elaborately—
    pea salad with blanched red onions, radishes and asparagus,
scalloped potatoes, all good things that come from the ground.

He eats the mini eggs I've left for guests until they're gone;
    he says, *How do you feel about abortion?*

I explain how you can eat violets, and dandelions, and wild chives,
so that we almost have an edible lawn. He says he hates birds.

I laugh and ask him, *How can you hate birds?*

He says he hates them because they're everywhere, they are all over,
everywhere you look, and we look up at the sky together.

Turns out he's right, those damn things are everywhere.

THE LAST DROP

You've just left your dad in Virginia with your brother after taking him to the neurologist to confirm that it is, in fact, Alzheimer's. Now, you're driving to New York to get your dead ex-girlfriend's cats who need a home and even though we weren't planning on cats, they're fifteen and who's gonna take them and you know them already and why not give some animals a home even if it's another twenty hours of driving there and back? I tell Manuel about your travels and he says, *It's a good premise for a horrible road trip dark comedy movie.* And there is something funny about it all. Your father hates cats, but they love him. And I spent a long time envious of your ex-girlfriend's beauty and now I only miss her and want to love her cats for her. My memoir could be titled *Everything Was Fine until It Wasn't*. My memoir could be called *I Thought I Wanted a Baby but All I Got Was Your Dead Ex-Girlfriend's Two Old Cats*. My memoir could be called *Before the Wedding You Must Suffer a Little*. My mother's motto is "Nothing Is Easy" and I tease her for it, but it's true. Before he left, your dad said he didn't understand the saying "Good to the last drop." *Does that mean the last drop is bad?* he asked. *No,* I reassured. *It means all of it is good, every single drop of it is good.*

from THE HURTING KIND

GIVE ME THIS

I thought it was the neighbor's cat, back
to clean the clock of the fledgling robins low
in their nest stuck in the dense hedge by the house,
but what came was much stranger, a liquidity
moving, all muscle and bristle: a groundhog
slippery and waddle-thieving my tomatoes, still
green in the morning's shade. I watched her
munch and stand on her haunches, taking such
pleasure in the watery bites. Why am I not allowed
delight? A stranger writes to request my thoughts
on suffering. Barbed wire pulled out of the mouth,
as if demanding that I kneel to the trap of coiled
spikes used in warfare and fencing. Instead,
I watch the groundhog more closely and a sound escapes
me, a small spasm of joy I did not imagine
when I woke. She is a funny creature and earnest,
and she is doing what she can to survive.

SANCTUARY

Suppose it's easy to slip
        into another's green skin,
bury yourself in leaves

and wait for a breaking,
        a breaking open, a breaking
out. I have, before, been

tricked into believing
        I could be both an I
and the world. The great eye

of the world is both gaze
        and gloss. To be swallowed
by being seen. A dream.

To be made whole
        by being not a witness,
but witnessed.

A GOOD STORY

Some days—dishes piled in the sink, books littering the coffee table—
are harder than others. Today, my head is packed with cockroaches,

dizziness, and everywhere it hurts. Venom in the jaw, behind the eyes,
between the blades. Still, the dog is snoring on my right, the cat, on my left.

Outside, all those redbuds are just getting good. I tell a friend, *The body
is so body*. And she nods. I used to like the darkest stories, the bleak

snippets someone would toss out about just how bad it could get.
My stepfather told me a story about when he lived on the streets as a kid,

how he'd, some nights, sleep under the grill at a fast food restaurant until
both he and his buddy got fired. I used to like that story for some reason,

something in me that believed in overcoming. But right now all I want
is a story about human kindness, the way once, when I couldn't stop

crying because I was fifteen and heartbroken, he came in and made
me eat a small pizza he'd cut up into tiny bites until the tears stopped.

Maybe I was just hungry, I said. And he nodded, holding out the last piece.

FORSYTHIA

At the cabin in Snug Hollow near McSwain Branch creek, just spring, all the animals are out, and my beloved and I are lying in bed in a soft silence. We are talking about how we carry so many people with us wherever we go, how, even when simply living, these unearned moments are a tribute to the dead. We are both expecting to hear an owl as the night deepens. All afternoon, from the porch, we watched an Eastern towhee furiously build her nest in the untamed forsythia with its yellow spilling out into the horizon. I told him that the way I remember the name *forsythia* is that when my stepmother, Cynthia, was dying, that last week, she said lucidly but mysteriously, *More yellow*. And I thought yes, more yellow, and nodded because I agreed. Of course, more yellow. And so now in my head, when I see that yellow tangle, I say, *For Cynthia, for Cynthia, forsythia, forsythia, more yellow*. It is night now, and the owl never comes. Only more of night, and what repeats in the night.

AND, TOO, THE FOX

Comes with its streak of red
flashing across the lawn, squirrel
bound and bouncing almost
as if it were effortless to hunt,
food being an afterthought or
just a little boring. He doesn't
say a word. Just uses those four
black feet to silently go about
his work, which doesn't seem
like work at all but play. Fox
lives on the edges, pieces together
a living out of leftovers and lazy
rodents too slow for the telephone
pole. He takes only what he needs
and lives a life that some might
call small, has a few friends, likes
the grass when it's soft and green,
never cares how long you watch,
never cares what you need
when you're watching, never cares
what you do once he is gone.

THE MAGNIFICENT FRIGATEBIRD

Is it okay to begin with the obvious? I am full of stones—
      is it okay not to look out this window, but to look out another?

A mentor once said, *You can't start a poem with a man looking*
      out a window. Too many men looking out a window.

What about a woman? Today is a haunting. One last orange
      on the counter: it is a dead fruit. We swallow dead things.

Once, in Rio near Leblon, large seabirds soared over the vast
      South Atlantic Ocean. I had never seen them before.

Eight-foot wingspan and gigantic in their confident gliding, black,
      with a red neck like a wound or a hidden treasure. Or both.

When I looked it up, I learned it was the Magnificent Frigatebird.
      It sounded like that enormity of a bird had named itself.

What a pleasure to say, *I am Magnificent*. And, too, they traveled as a team,
      so I wondered if they named each other. Generously tapping

one another's deeply forked tail or their plumage, glistening with salt air,
      their gular sacs saying, *You are Magnificent. You are also Magnificent.*

It makes me want to give all my loves the adjectives they deserve:
      You are Resplendent. You are Radiant. You are Sublime.

I am far away from tropical waters. I have no skills for flight or wings
      to skim the waves effortlessly, like the wind itself. But from here,

I can still imagine rapture, a glorious caught fish in the mouth of a bird.

THE FIRST FISH

When I pulled that great fish up out of Lake Skinner's
    mirrored-double surface, I wanted to release
the tugging beast immediately. Disaster on the rod,
    it seemed he might yank the whole aluminum skiff
down toward the bottom of his breathless world.
    The old tree of a man yelled to hang on and would
not help me as I reeled and reeled, finally seeing
    the black carp come up to meet me, black eye
to black eye. In the white cooler it looked so impossible.
    Is this where I am supposed to apologize? Not
only to the fish, but to the whole lake, land, not only for me
    but for the generations of plunder and vanish.
I remember his terrible mouth opening as if to swallow
    the barbarous girl he'd lose his life to. That gold-ringed
eye did not pardon me, no absolution, no reprieve.
    I wanted to catch something; it wanted to live.
We never ate the bottom-feeder, buried by the rosebush
    where my ancestors swore the roses bloomed
twice as big that year, the year I killed a thing because
    I was told to, the year I met my twin and buried
him without weeping so I could be called brave.

JOINT CUSTODY

Why did I never see it for what it was:
abundance? Two families, two different
kitchen tables, two sets of rules, two
creeks, two highways, two stepparents
with their fish tanks or eight-tracks or
cigarette smoke or expertise in recipes or
reading skills. I cannot reverse it, the record
scratched and stopping to that original
chaotic track. But let me say, I was taken
back and forth on Sundays and it was not easy
but I was loved each place. And so I have
two brains now. Two entirely different brains.
The one that always misses where I'm not,
and the one that is so relieved to finally be home.

CYRUS & THE SNAKES

My brother holds a snake by its head. The whole
    length of the snake is the length

of my brother's body. The snake's head
    is held safely, securely, as if my brother

is showing it something in the distant high grass.
    I don't know why he wants to hold them,

their strong bodies wrapping themselves around
    the warmth of his arm. Constricting and made

of circles and momentum; slippery coolness smooth
    against the ground. Still, this image of him,

holding a snake as it snakes as snakes
    do, both a noun and a verb and a story

that doesn't end well. Once, we stole an egg
    from the backyard chicken coop

and cracked it just to see what was inside: a whole
    unhatched chick. Where we

expected yolk and mucus was an unfeathered
    and unfurled sweetness. We stared at the thing,

dead now and unshelled by curiosity and terrible youth.
    My brother pretended not to care so much,

while I cried, though only a little. Still, we buried it
    in the brush, by the creeping thistle that tore up

our arms with their speared leaves, barbed
>   at the ends like weapons stuck in the rattlesnake grass.

But I knew, I knew that he'd cry if he was alone,
>   if he wasn't a boy in the summer heat being a boy

in the summer heat. Years later, back from Mexico
>   or South America, he'd admit he was tired

of history, of always discovering the ruin by ruining
>   it, wrecking a forest for a temple, a temple

that should be simply left a temple. He wanted it
>   all to stay as it was, even if it went undiscovered.

I want to honor a man who wants to hold a wild thing,
>   only for a second, long enough to admire it fully,

and then wants to watch it safely return to its life,
>   bends to be sure the grass closes up behind it.

CALLING THINGS WHAT THEY ARE

I pass the feeder and yell, *Grackle party!* And then an hour later I yell, *Mourning dove afterparty!* (I call the feeder the party and the seed on the ground the afterparty.) I am getting so good at watching that I've even dug out the binoculars an old poet gave me back when I was young and heading to the Cape with so much future ahead of me it was like my own ocean. *Tufted titmouse!* I yell, and Lucas laughs and says, *Thought so.* But he is humoring me; he didn't think so at all. My father does this same thing. Shouts out at the feeder announcing the party attendees. He throws out a whole peanut or two to the Steller's jay who visits on a low oak branch in the morning. To think there was a time I thought birds were kind of boring. Brown bird. Gray bird. Black bird. Blah blah blah bird. Then, I started to learn their names by the ocean, and the person I was dating said, *That's the problem with you, Limón, you're all fauna and no flora.* And I began to learn the names of trees. I like to call things as they are. Before, the only thing I was interested in was love, how it grips you, how it terrifies you, how it annihilates and resuscitates you. I didn't know then that it wasn't even love that I was interested in but my own suffering. I thought suffering kept things interesting. How funny that I called it love and the whole time it was pain.

OPEN WATER

It does no good to trick and weave and lose
the other ghosts, to shove the buried deeper
into the sandy loam, the riverine silt; still you come,
my faithful one, the sound of a body so persistent
in water I cannot tell if it is a wave or you
moving through. A month before you died
you wrote a letter to old friends saying you swam
with a pod of dolphins in open water, saying goodbye,
but what you told me most about was the eye.
That enormous reckoning eye of an unknown fish
that passed you during that last-ditch defiant swim.
On the shore, you described the fish as nothing
you'd seen before, a blue-gray behemoth moving slowly
and enduringly through its deep fathomless
North Pacific waters. That night, I heard more
about that fish and that eye than anything else.
I don't know why it has come to me this morning.
Warm rain and landlocked, I don't deserve the image.
But I keep thinking how something saw you, something
was bearing witness to you out there in the ocean
where you were no one's mother, and no one's wife,
but you in your original skin; right before you died,
you were beheld, and today in my kitchen with you
now ten years gone, I am so happy for you.

PRIVACY

On the black wet branches of the linden,
still clinging to the umber leaves of late fall,
two crows land. They say, *Stop*, and still I want
to make them into something they are not.
Odin's ravens, the bruja's eyes. What news
are they bringing of our world to the world
of the gods? It can't be good. More suffering
all around, more stinging nettles and toxic
blades shoved into the scarred parts of us,
the minor ones underneath the trees. Rain
comes while I'm still standing, a trickle of water
from whatever we believe is beyond the sky.
The crows seem enormous but only because
I am watching them too closely. They do not
care to be seen as symbols. A shake of a wing,
and both of them are gone. There was no message
given, no message I was asked to give, only
their great absence and my sad privacy
returning like the bracing, empty wind
on the black wet branches of the linden.

SPORTS

I've seen my fair share of baseball games,
eaten smothered hot dogs in Kansas City
and carne asada burritos in San Francisco
in the sunny stands on a day free of fog.
I've sat in a bar for hours watching
basketball and baseball and the Super Bowl,
and I've even high-fived and clinked
my almost-empty drink with a stranger
because it felt good to go through something
together even though we hadn't been through
anything but the drama of a game, its players.
If I am honest, what I love, why I love
the sounds of the games even when I'm not
interested, half-listening, is one thing:
When my father and my stepfather had to be
in the same room, or had to drop my brother
and me off during our weekly move from one
house to another, they, for a brief moment,
would stand together in the doorway or
on the gravel driveway and it felt like what true
terror should feel like, two men who were so
different you could barely see their shadows
attached in the same way, and just when
I thought I couldn't watch the pause
lengthen between them, they'd talk about
the playoffs or the finals or whatever team
was doing whatever thing required that season
and sometimes they'd even shrug or make
a motion that felt like two people who weren't
opposites after all. Once, I sat in the car
and waited for one of them to take me away

and from the back seat I swear they looked
like they were on the same team, united
against a common enemy, had been fighting,
all this time, on the same side.

PROOF

A kestrel eyes us from a high thin branch
and my husband is surprised it can hold the hunter's
weight. *He's small*, I say. My husband says he's large.
Obviously, it depends on what you compare him to—
a hawk, a white-crowned sparrow, a ghost,
an abstraction. He looms not large to me, but significant.
A standout. Something cool about him that says today
is the day to test his mettle in the mid-morning air,
flush with dead leaves and the ongoingness of rusted
mums. A surge of relief comes like a check in the mail.
Look, I have already witnessed something other than my
slipping face in the fogged mirror, the dog's sweet
seriousness at being worshipped from nose to paw.
I have proof a nearly twiglike branch can still hold
a too-heavy falcon. It is not much to go on, I know.

HEART ON FIRE

As a foster child, my grandfather learned not
to get in trouble. Mexican and motherless—dead
as she was from tuberculosis—he practiced words
in a new language and kept his slender head down.
When the other boys begged him to slip into
the music shop's upper window to steal harmonicas
for each of them, music being important, thievery
being secondary, he refused. When the cops came
to spot the boys who robbed the music store, they
could easily find the ones spitting broken
notes into the air, joyously mouthing the stainless
steel, mimicking men on street corners busking
for coins. But not my grandfather, he knew not
to risk it all for a stolen moment of exultation.
It's easy to imagine this is who I come from, a line
of serious men who follow the rules, but might I add
that later he was a dancer, a singer, an actor whose best roles
ended up on the cutting room floor. A cutup, a ham
who liked a good story. Who would have told you
life was a series of warnings, but also magic. Once,
he was sent for a box of matches and he put that box
of strike-anywheres in the pocket of his madras shirt
and ran home, he ran so fast to be on time, to be good,
and when he did so, the whole box ignited, so he was
a boy running down the canyon road with what
looked like a heart on fire. He'd laugh when he told
you this, *a heart on fire*, he'd say, so you'd remember.

MY FATHER'S MUSTACHE

Let us pause to applaud the white bell-bottom suit,
the wide flared collar, the black thick-coiffed hair
in this photo my father has sent of himself
at a gathering off Sonoma Highway in the early '70s.
I can't stop looking at the photo. There is a swagger
that feels almost otherworldly, epic, like Lorca
expounding in Buenos Aires, *Not the form
but the marrow of form.* He is perfect there, my father
in the photo. I feel somehow as if I'm perched on a bay laurel
branch nearby though not born yet. It's in black and white, the photo.
You can see his grin behind his lush mustache. Is it time
that moves in me now? A sense of ache and unraveling,
my father in his pristine white suit, the eye of the world barely able
to handle his smooth unbroken stride. It's been a year
since I've seen him in person, I miss how he points
to his apple trees and I miss his smooth face
that no longer has the mustache I always adored.
As a child I once cried when he shaved it. Even then,
I was too attached to this life.

THE HURTING KIND

1.

On the plane I have a dream I've left half my
       torso on the back porch with my beloved. I have to go

back for it, but it's too late, I'm flying
       and there's only half of me.

Back in Texas, the flowers I've left on
       the counter (I stay alone there so the flowers
are more than flowers) have wilted and knocked over the glass.

At the funeral parlor with my mother, we are holding her father's suit,
       and she says, *He'll swim in these.*

For a moment, I'm not sure what she means,

until I realize she means the clothes are too big.

I go with her like a shield in case they try to upsell her
       the ridiculously ornate urn, the elaborate body box.

It is a nice bathroom in the funeral parlor,
       so I take the opportunity to change my tampon.

When I come out my mother says,
Did you have to change your tampon?

And it seems, all at once, a vulgar life. Or not
       vulgar, but not simple, either.

I'm driving her now to Hillside Cemetery where we meet
      with Rosie, who is so nice we want her to work
everywhere. Rosie as my dentist. Rosie as my president.

My shards are showing, I think. But I do not know what I mean
so I fix my face in the rearview, a face with thousands
      of headstones behind it. Minuscule flags, plastic flowers.

      You can't sum it up, my mother says as we are driving,
and the electronic voice says, *Turn left onto Wildwood Canyon Road*,

so I turn left, happy for the instructions.

Tell me where to go. Tell me how to get there.

She means a life, of course. You cannot sum it up.

2.

A famous poet said he never wanted to hear
another poem about a grandmother or a grandfather.

I imagine him with piles of faded yolk-colored paper,
overloaded with loops of swooping cursive, anemic lyrics

misspelling *mourning* and *morning*. But also, before they arrive,
there's a desperate hand scribbling a memory, following

the cat of imagination into each room. What is lineage,
if not a gold thread of pride and guilt? *She did what?*

Once, when I thought I had decided not to have children,
a woman said, *But who are you to kill your own bloodline?*

I told my friend D that, and she said, *What if you want to kill your own bloodline, like it's your job?*

In the myth of La Llorona, she drowns her children
to destroy her cheating husband. But maybe she was just tired.

After her husband of seventy-six years has died, my grandmother
(yes, I said it, *grandmother, grandmother*) leans to me and says,

Now teach me poetry.

3.

Sticky packs of photographs,
heteromaniacal postcards.

The war.   The war.   The war.
Bikini girls, tight curls, the word *gams*.

Land boom. Atchison, Topeka,
and the Santa Fe. Southern Pacific.

We ask my grandma Allamay
about her mother, for a form.

Records and wills. Evidence of life.
For a moment she can't remember
her mother's maiden name.

She says, *Just tell them she never
wanted me. That should be enough.*

*Red sadness is the secret
one*, writes Ruefle. Redlands

was named after the soil.
Allamay can still
hold a peach in her hand

and judge its number by
its size. Tell you where it
would go in the box

if you're packing peaches
for a living. Which she did,

though she hated the way
the hairs hurt her hands.

4.

Why do we quickly dismiss our ancient ones? Before our phones
    stole the light of our faces, shiny and blue in the televised night,

they worked farms and butchered and trapped animals and swept houses
    and returned to each other after long hours and told stories.

In order for someone to be "good" do they have to have
    seen the full-tilt world? Must they believe what we believe?

My grandmother keeps a picture of her president in the top drawer
    of her dresser, and once, when she was delusional, she dreamt

he had sent my grandfather and her on a trip to Italy. *He paid for it all*,
    she kept repeating.

That same night, on her ride to the hospital, she talks to the medical
    technician and says,

All my grandchildren are Mexican.

She says so proudly; she repeats it to me on the phone.

5.

Once, a long time ago, we sat in the carport of my grandparents'
    house in Redlands, now stolen by eminent domain,

now the hospital parking lot, no more coyotes or caves
    where the coyotes would live, or the grandfather clock

in the house my grandfather built, the porch above the orchard,
    all gone.

We sat in the carport and watched the longest snake
    I'd ever seen undulate between the hanging succulents.

They told me not to worry, that the snake had a name,

    the snake was called a California king,

all slick black with yellow
    stripes like wonders wrapping around him.

My grandparents, my ancestors, told me never
    to kill a California king, benevolent

as they were, equanimous like earth or sky, not

    toothy like the dog Chacho who barked
at nearly every train whistle or roadrunner.

Before my grandfather died, I asked him what sort
    of horse he had growing up. He said,

Just a horse. My horse, with such a tenderness it
    rubbed the bones in my ribs all wrong.

I have always been too sensitive, a weeper
    from a long line of weepers.

I am the hurting kind. I keep searching for proof.

My grandfather carried that snake to the cactus,
    where all sharp things could stay safe.

6.

You can't sum it up. A life.

I feel it moving through me, that snake,
    his horse Midge sturdy and nothing special,

traveling the canyons and the tumbleweeds
    hunting for rabbits before the war.

My grandmother picking peaches. Stealing
    the fruit from the orchards as she walked

home. No one said it was my job to remember.

    I took no notes, though I've stared too long.
My grandfather, before he died, would have told

    anyone that could listen that he was ordinary,

that his life was a good one, simple, he could never
> understand why anyone would want to write

it down. He would tell you straight up he wasn't
> brave. And my grandmother would tell you right now

that he is busy getting the house ready for her. Visiting now
each night and even doing the vacuuming.

I imagine she's right. It goes on and on, their story.
> They met in first grade in a one-room schoolhouse,

I could have started their story there, but it
> is endless and ongoing. All of this

is a conjuring. I will not stop this reporting of attachments.
> There is evidence everywhere.

There's a tree over his grave now, and soon her grave too

> though she is tough and says, *If I ever die,*

which is marvelous and maybe why she's still alive.

I see the tree above the grave and think, *I'm wearing*

my heart on my leaves. My heart on my leaves.

Love ends. But what if it doesn't?

AGAINST NOSTALGIA

If I had known, back then, you were coming,
when I first thought love could be the thing
to save me after all—if I had known, would I
have still glued myself to the back of his
motorcycle while we flew across the starless
bridge over the East River to where I grew
my first garden behind the wire fencing,
in the concrete raised beds lined by ruby
twilight roses? If I had known it would be you,
who even then I liked to look at, across a room,
always listening rigorously, a self-questioning look,
the way your mouth was always your mouth,
would I have climbed back on that bike again
and again until even I was sick with fumes
and the sticky seat too hot in the early fall?
If I had known, would I have still made mistake
after mistake until I had only the trunk of me
left, stripped and nearly bare of leaves?
If I had known, the truth is, I would have kneeled
and said, *Sooner, come to me sooner.*

SALVAGE

On the top of Mount Pisgah, on the western
slope of the Mayacamas, there's a madrone
tree that's half-burned from the fires, half-alive
from nature's need to propagate. One side
of her is black ash, and at her root is what
looks like a cavity hollowed out by flame.
On the other side, silvery-green broadleaf
shoots ascend toward the winter light
and her bark is a cross between a bay
horse and a chestnut horse, red and velvety
like the animal's neck she resembles. Staring
at the tree for a long time now, I am reminded
of the righteousness I had before the scorch
of time. I miss who I was. I miss who we all were,
before we were this: half-alive to the brightening sky,
half-dead already. I place my hand on the unscarred
bark that is cool and unsullied, and because I cannot
apologize to the tree, to my own self I say, *I am sorry.
I am sorry I have been so reckless with your life.*

THE END OF POETRY

Enough of osseous and chickadee and sunflower
and snowshoes, maple and seeds, samara and shoot,
enough chiaroscuro, enough of thus and prophecy
and the stoic farmer and faith and our father and 'tis
of thee, enough of bosom and bud, skin and god
not forgetting and star bodies and frozen birds,
enough of the will to go on and not go on or how
a certain light does a certain thing, enough
of the kneeling and the rising and the looking
inward and the looking up, enough of the gun,
the drama, and the acquaintance's suicide, the long-lost
letter on the dresser, enough of the longing and
the ego and the obliteration of ego, enough
of the mother and the child and the father and the child
and enough of the pointing to the world, weary
and desperate, enough of the brutal and the border,
enough of can you see me, can you hear me, enough
I am human, enough I am alone and I am desperate,
enough of the animal saving me, enough of the high
water, enough sorrow, enough of the air and its ease,
I am asking you to touch me.

STARTLEMENT

NEW POEMS

THE ENDLESSNESS

At first I was lonely, but then I was
curious. The original fault was that I could
not see the lines of things. My mother could.
She could see shapes and lines and shadows,
but all I could see was memory, what had been
done to the object before it was placed on
the coffee table or the nightstand. I could sense
that it had a life underneath it. Because
of this, I thought I was perhaps bad at seeing. Even
color was not color, but a mood. The lamp was
sullen, a candlestick brooding and rude with its old
wax crumbling at its edges, not flame, not a promise
of flame. How was I supposed to feel then? About
moving in the world? How could I touch anything
or anyone without the weight of all of time shifting
through us? I was not, or I did not think I was, making
up stories; it was how the world was, or rather it is how
the world is. I've only now become better at pretending
that there are edges, boundaries, that if I touch
something it cannot always touch me back.

HELL OR HIGH WATER

Not churchgoers or joiners, still my people sang,
up Highway 12 or Arnold Drive, depending
on the traffic. "Blue moon, you saw me standing
alone," my maternal grandfather would croon
in a big put-on cowboy voice like Marty Robbins
as we barreled up the 79 from Julian to Calimesa
after all their money disappeared in a savings-
and-loan scam and they lost everything they
thought was safe come hell or high water. On
the other side, el otro lado, my grandfather would
sing Lydia Mendoza rancheras and "Mal Hombre,"
songs about la frontera, on our way from Oceanside
to Laguna Beach. Also here, in the mountains,
I remember driving up from Glen Ellen, the drive
interminable, my brother's pugilistic tendencies bruising
me on the back seat's sticky vinyl; even then, we
could be swayed to sing. At the campsite, my
father would pull out his guitar, and we'd beg
him for "The Cat Came Back" or "500 Miles," something
with a chorus we could sing along to, sometimes
we'd even like the sad songs. Drifting to black
between the flames of the fire, and the aspen
and the pines all flickering in the distance. What
was the difference between a song sung on
the journey and a song sung once you got there,
one was about passing the time, the other about
bellowing your presence to the rocks and stones,
I don't know. I know that we sang, and here in this
valley I can't help but think of how my father pulled
out his guitar at my stepmother's deathbed, which
was just their bed really, at home up north and on a cold
clear day he sang "500 Miles," and she was already

almost gone and I wept and his voice sounded so strong
so when the hospice nurse came and said, "You
have no religion, right?" I didn't know how to answer,
because we did, it was this, it was all those years
tied together on the road, singing at the tops of our
lungs, harmonious and inharmonious both, and with gusto,
our voices meshed together like tree roots, not for any
good reason other than the sheer pleasure of it,
something to pass the time, like beauty, like going
to the mountaintop just to go, it's the old way,
it's the only way I know, a mountain, an echo,
a coming back and coming back, a chorus.

WHILE EVERYTHING ELSE WAS FALLING APART

In the Union Square subway station nearly fifteen
years ago now, the L train came clanking by
where someone had fat-Sharpied a black heart
on the yellow pillar you leaned on during a bleak day
(brittle and no notes from anyone you crushed upon).
Above ground, the spring sun was the saddest one
(doing work, but also none). What were you wearing?
Something hopeful to show the world you hoped?
A tall man was learning from a vendor how to pronounce
churro. High in the sticky clouds of time, he kept
repeating churro while eating a churro. How to say
this made you want to live? No hand to hold,
still here it was: someone giving someone comfort
and someone memorizing hard how to ask for it again.

STRANGE REFUGE

Above the low and pillared Mississippi skyline,
    some blue, blue twilight and one star is blinking back

at this hotel window. I am in the window's reflection,
    so I am also in the sky, a fake blue blouse under

the real blue, the singular star fading under
    a contrail or a cloud, I am figuring out my face:

It is me, and it is not me. A reconfiguration of all
    my faces. Blank cynical glare of the brooding

girl who couldn't keep all the stones she thumbed
    until she wished not to part with the gray,

the one with the rivulet of chert, sweet greed between
    the eyes. And here now, I'm out of focus

and blinking and it feels better than any clarity,
    nothing sticks on a movement, a gesture

from a distance. Under the star, one tall pine. *You
    are far away from home*, something says

when the hotel heat comes on. I play a song
    and sing along. The star is gone, everything

has faded, now it's more me in the glass, too much
    of me and even the song is ending.

What if this one in the window—huzzah,
    spells and such—is who I am, not the mind

in the pine needles or the pitch changes,
    not even the stones I couldn't keep,

or what if I did keep them, all this time, here
    in this reflection where I am opening my hand?

THIS ONE GOES OUT TO

Lakeside martini with four olives and an attitude
    and someone talked about how many times

we've been sat in the corner when a good table
    came and went, our dads scowling, and we howled

in laughter, the best medicine they say, future
    is a tough thing to value, orbital pulse

of what's to come, who has a view, who can see
    from this pleasant distance,

the rising tide and the bank statement? I press
    myself into an envelope and wonder at what

legacy means, lean deep into oh my god, we are all,
    I dunno, mortal. I am thinking of a man I dated

once and he said I looked great and I said thank you
    and later he said I should never just say thank you

because it was rude. He was the same man who once
    asked if I wanted to watch a three-hour concert

of himself on the TV in his living room, don't worry, he offered
    to order food, the cojones, this cocky friend,

so I left through a hole in my sweater and went back
    to those restaurants that our fathers fought

for, so odd to think it matters, but I remember
    the secret tips, the nods, the I will not be sat

by the kitchen goddamn it, I will not be sat by
         the bathroom, even if I am the help, even

if I wait tables at the next spot over, you will
         carve a space for me where I can see

the lake, the clouds, the thing everyone is here for
         and I will find pleasure, my pleasure—

this one goes out to
this one goes out to
this one goes out to

—in my loudness, in my otherness, in my anesthetized
         pain, I'll shove all of this in my mouth.

Loudly, brightly, my risky ease drips through
         the generations, flick of a wrist, raise a glass,

laugh until admonishment, you're in the good seat,
         for one hot minute, pardon me,

who's in charge here?

FIELD

Love is the revelation of the other person's freedom. —Octavio Paz

To consider him with horses is to consider him
as himself. He doesn't notice much else—
the business of mud swallows, the drenched grass
soaking his jeans and field boots—but the way a yearling
begs his attention or a barren mare bares her teeth
into what looks like a grin. He sees each luminescent
hair, the light making waves on a bay stallion's coat,
and I try to renounce my boredom, my envy. He loves
him some horses. Horses, horses, horses. All my life,
people I love have been pointing at horses. I met a great
poet once, and all he wanted to talk about was my
husband and horses. He said when he was growing up
he'd send away for those slick-paged horse catalogs
to stare at pictures of equine standouts. Strange, but to love
my love is to love horses, how they run, how they burst
into a field in a frenzy, their long strides, their strong will
and unwillingness. I've given up on wanting to own
his two eyes for only myself. I used to think the horse
was my double, bravado and bristle, but that was
a falsehood, it was always him, from forelock to fetlock,
standing in a field, waiting for me to call him home.

MORTALITY

When a poet says, "Let me
be clear," we are never clear.

Big drops on the palm fronds
and a fat moon under clouds.

Language, I love it, but it is of the air
and we are of the earth.

I want you to know this image—
plumeria wet and swaying,

but only the sound of a door
closing in an empty room comes,

something beginning and ending
without so much as a warning.

SEA TURTLE

First it was a rock
then not a rock at all.

First there was only water
then shadow pushing

against water—then
a head, a front fin,

the hard carapace,
and together we

were swimming, at ease,
no hurry, no rules.

Later, I pretended he
saw me, that he was closer

than he was. It is in my
nature to tell stories,

to tell you what he meant
serene and excellent

and how he mirrored my
desire with a sort of un-desire,

but what is more true
is that I laughed, ridiculous

joy, seeing his head arise
and disappear and arise

again. Joy didn't feel heavy
enough for such a stately

creature of ages. I kept
my distance and laughed

and pointed and was full
of surprise and the best part?

Every sound I made
disappeared in the waves.

CROW'S-FEET

Flooded wetlands, pounded by
more rain, no birds, no signs

of anything, I'm holding some wild
idea of unity, conviction, like a jar

of pollywogs, so carefully carried,
so full of potential, live, live, I say

quietly to the jar, which isn't a jar
but my own pounding invocation,

I am not fading, but becoming
ungovernable. This train keeps

boasting its speed, the conductor
says, *May you have a great day,*

on purpose. On purpose hangs
in the car, all of us ransacked

by the bidding, watching our
faces be carried away and fast.

LET LOOSE

The soft low voice instructs me to breathe
with gusto and return to the body. The body,
it posits, is safe, it is grounding, it is different
than the skittering mind. The nerves between
my spine and ribs are screeching, gnawing,
playing a sick game of cringe roulette and I'm
losing. A long breath aches, a rib flinches
as if it's a dog about to be hit, the drench
of claws, not a fever, but a wincing of the skin,
and so let me, I beg of you, let me return
to the cool safety of the mind. I stand in defense
of the mind. My own crass and psychedelic
vivacity. The mind that wanders, that illuminates
this quaking aspen, this sugar pine, this ponderosa,
and imagines lying against the icy grass, imagines
each trembling green blade soothing nerve endings,
every too-alive glial cell coming to heel. The watery
voice again swears the body will bring a sense of ease,
but roughed up, I'm already on the gondola gliding
up the mountain shedding each part of my skinned
self as I go. There, a limb, there, a nervous system,
anything that yowls is let loose, watch each part
of me released and become something entirely
acrobatic and weightless, not flying, but not falling
just entirely in love with the air, oh look at how
gorgeous I am! Falling away from myself, no body
at all, just the mountain, just the breath
of the mountain, no not even the breath
of the mountain, nothing that can be hurt, or taken,
nothing that can be broken into or scarred,
something invisible and just how I imagined.

HOW TO MEASURE DISTANCE

1.

Under the sculpted buttocks

    of Michelangelo's David

we stand and marvel at the marble

    statue, the veins in the legs, the miracle

of the human form. Each of us has forgotten

    that this David is the David that fought

Goliath. Took a stone and knocked flat the giant.

    How huge he looks now in the museum's light,

but how trapped in endless tourism. Someone mentions

he needs to be freed, adored and worshipped

    in the real light of trees.

2.

In the cramped bathroom rank

    with the ages, the back of the door

is scratched full of cryptic and not-so cryptic

scrawls. One says, "Remember you are

beautiful." And next to that one, "David could

    slide into my DMs." In some distant part

of the mind, all those who ejected early from

    this earth come back and I think of them

feeling unworthy or exhausted or desperate

    for some new reality or at least the end

of this one. In tight penmanship that connotes

    a desperation, someone has written,

"Don't ever forget that you are loved." I think she

    means it as a note to herself or a note

to some future version of herself, don't forget

    don't forget.

3.

On the drive to yet another beautiful place

    (so pretty we could die), we realize

we still can't figure out kilometers. We are dumb

    Americans speeding into the golden light

of Tuscany. We decide then to measure distance by

    Davids. The restaurant is about fifty Davids

away. The castle bedroom is four Davids squared.

    For a brief moment, I visualize that every road

has marble Davids toe to head and head to toe

    lying perfectly together guiding everyone

toward some better human intention. Follow beauty

    or beware!

4.

Before we enter the room where he stood, T asks

    if I expect to be moved. I answer

that I always expect to be moved. And then there

    he is and I remember that first time

I thought of the human body as perfect. It wasn't

    a man's or even someone else's but me at seventeen

in my apartment staring at my body, really looking

  in the mirror and for once not hating myself

but thinking that it was all miraculous, fingers,

  feet, flaws which were not flaws at all but curiosities.

Who was Goliath then? Who else but my own mind,

  the voice that told me I was all wrong, awkward,

unwanted, undesired, too round, and then, I stared

  in that mirror and I decided I'd throw stones

at that monster for the rest of my life.

5.

There are replicas everywhere of the statue,

  and so from a pink shell-shaped seat, we stare

at another David, next to what we have come to call

  the worried lions. (So worried!) Gruesome statues

too, a head ripped off, the insides of man and monster

  spilling out underneath the blue light of clouds.

Isn't that how it is? Beauty up against everything we know.

  And so you find something so perfectly made

you try to repeat it until every shop window

      has 1,000 tiny Davids waiting to be carried home

or broken or sat to rest under a sycamore

      until vines cover him up. But still there are more

to be made, and so what, go ahead and make more,

      carry them in the mind's eye, in this pocket

of history, like a type of scripture, a grandiose story

      of some improbable myth, a blue pen

on the bathroom wall saying, "Don't forget, don't forget."

LITERARY THEORY

Somehow the word
allow is in the word
swallow and in *swallow*
two wholly different meanings:
one to take in through
the mouth and another
what we call the common
winged gnat hunter who
is, in all probability,
somewhere near us now.
Once, I thought
if I knew all the words
I would say the right thing
in the right way,
instead language became
more brutish: blink twice
for the bird, blink once
for tender annihilation. Who
knows what we are doing as
we go about our days lazily
choosing our languages. Some
days my life is held together
by definitions, some days
I read the word *swallow*
and all my feathers show.

EVEN HERE IT IS HAPPENING

And so I iron the dress,
        the steamed wool smelling
of schoolboys in the always-falling rain.

It's mustard color, the dress—
I must wear it like a uniform.

Sometimes someone sees
a loneliness in me, but what

        it is is a need to be alone, out
there—out there falling in gray air.

The clouds aren't clean, covering
        for smoke, yet we point to clouds
as if it is our job. Oh god,

what if all I've done is guard
myself against despair?

THE GEOGRAPHY OF MOUNTAINS

In the center of the center, somehow another
    center. I wake in the valley with a view
    of a blue shed in a green field.

A round picture of a hummingbird recalls a clock
    without hands—and so always
    it's hummingbird time.

(A swish of minutes. A revolve of wings.)

No one believes that people just point
    to the moon, but I just said,
    "Look! The moon!" And we all looked.

Growing up, I could see San Pablo Bay from Moon Mountain,
    and Mount Tamalpais,
    they'd say, "Mount Tamalpais looks like a woman sleeping."

The problem? All mountains look like women sleeping to me.
    The body's curves, the flood
    of hair, the releasing into the earth, somnolence at last.

I want to be sleeping like those mountains, lazy as the laziest
    days of summer, too lazy to even lick the popsicle stick,
    just anchored in the understory.

Everyone wants you to rest, but they, too,
    want you to return their notes with some urgency,
    they say, "Please take it easy, but after
    you take care of this, for me."

Once my mother pulled me out of school
>   and I sobbed because I was going to miss
>   so much and then, god forbid,

I'd be given a B and she said that's why
>   I needed a break from school, to know it was okay to be idle,
>   I was in third grade.

In college, I wrote a paper on Wittgenstein
>   and got his whole theory about God wrong,
>   but managed to earn a B because even though I had missed the point,

the paper was well written and contained dreams.
>   I am always missing the point, I want
>   to sit for a long time and not be in pain. I said to someone

recently, *I'd like to have all pictures taken of me
>   taken lying down*, it seemed
>   like a perfectly fine figure, a portrait

of a woman resting, everything

around her coming to a stop, a hummingbird at the feeder,
>   not in any hurry, a slow motion to grace,
>   the blade of a machine finally stuck

in the rock of the mountain, no dynamite,
>   all the world called off, sent home to rest, cessation,
>   and don't worry, the dead do not look

like they are napping, they look dead.

You cannot wake them, not even
> to ask for forgiveness or to be reminded
> of what they said so we don't go on getting it wrong.

But I love to see my people in repose,
> at ease, the siesta's long
> tradition, healing in the heat. When I sleep

I am so busy in my dreams that I wake
> and sometimes that too feels
> like rest. Wittgenstein said,

"We wake up sometimes, just to know we are dreaming."

After all these years, I am waking up.

After all these years, I've come home, to the valley,
> and now I know well the mountain that looks
> like a woman sleeping. I can point at her curves.

I know also that all mountains
> are women sleeping, dissolving imperceptibly,
> stretched out at last, alone, at rest,
> the source of everything.

CURTAIN CALL

She comes in already cold,
holding an apple. *Here is an apple*, she says.

Someone says, *But is it a real apple*
    or the performance of an apple?

Someone says, *If you can't eat it to survive, why*
    would I care?

Someone says, *Must be nice to be so philosophical*
    about war.

Let's not call it war, let's call it slaughter, she says
    and still offers the apple to the empty room.

I can't be trusted with this, says an echo
    and no one can tell if it's because of pleasure

(and pleasure is not allowed here) or because
    of violence (which is allowed).

She holds the apple and wants so much to
    believe in it. Its goodness.

Someone says, *Set it on fire and be done!*

She does not know if they mean the apple
    or her own self, which she has come to
equate with the apple.

She looks at the apple in her hand,
    there is no safe place for it. It can't

be offered or given anymore. It is real. And it's an idea.

She doesn't want it to die, she doesn't want anyone
    to be killed, not just children,

    but anyone, not the trees, not the water,
not the animals, which are also us. Animals.

Someone says, *I hope you choke on the apple.*

[Applause! Applause!]

(She thinks she's been standing too long.)

She can almost feel the apple lodged in her throat
    and thinks it might be safest there.

Does safety exist anywhere? Where is the knife
    pointed if not at the throat.

In small wincing bites, she begins to eat the apple,

she is crying now, but no one cares, nothing at all
    can be demolished in the body.

Instead it waits. She's struck at once

    by her own foolishness. The apple
doesn't solve anything, doesn't feed, or clothe, or bury,

instead it falls and falls from the tree,
        where more pointless fruit falls,
the bitter stems fractured over the ground

trying to remember their beginning, stems
        turning into something like a word.

EVERY BLOOMING THING

Shot out in the sun, those pink
blooms mouth the fall air
like needy fiends brightening
with desire. Long ago, before
I knew the difference between
skin sack and petal, I told my
parents I wanted to be a naked
lady. Those flamingo flowers
standing tall along the highways
and backroads. Even when all
the grass was gold and crisp
with flame danger, those lilies,
they never seemed to tire. Never
lost their surprise or their softness.
I didn't know then it was wrong
to wish to be a naked lady, wronger
even to wish to be a flower.

ON EARTH AS IT IS ON EARTH

Green and green and green, I speak
to the tree line, a booming body, trying
not to boom. I see myself as I once
was, hiding inside a manzanita outside
the ceramic studio, the mirrored rain-
drops hanging on urn-shaped blooms
and soon, too, my strands of hair. There was
always a line where the rain fell and where
it didn't. It was the line between abandonment
and freedom, loneliness and imagination.
How I waited in there, composing in my mind
a life without rules, without money, cruelty,
clocks, or clothes, how still I am the same,
in the green, in the green, waiting out the rain.

IN THE END, EVERYTHING GIVES

What is above us?
      The bleary algorithm of patterns, leaves,
           towering history of law and lore?

Outside the gates, the chaotic hush of flesh
      and bone, a kind of clamoring, cannon fire,
           or a brass band, a choir of tree limbs asking:

What have we made? Who holds you?

Where resides our genius? Our courageousness of action,
      name the glory, rename the glory, pin it down
           in a book of legacies, ink, and stone.

There is a word that returns to me: Realm.

      Someone on a train shrugs cartoonish,
      "What gives?" And the answer: Everything.

Everything gives way, the shorelines, the house decaying
      and becoming shrub and moss and haunt, the body
           that gives and gives until it cannot give anymore.

When sleepless as a child, my mother would draw my face,
      not with charcoal or oil paints, but with her fingers
           simply circling my features. Here are your eyes.

Here are your eyebrows, your nose, your mouth, your chin,
      and your whole face, round and round, this is you.

This was when I understood boundaries, that she could
    see my shapes, and I was made of circles and she
        was made of circles. All of us modest etchings

in the landscape, a fingernail dug into the side of a tree,
    little winces, let me count the ways, let me count the days,
        all the circles of us end eventually.

The light is its own story. When there is a hole in a roof,
    what is the roof, the roof or the sky itself? Maybe that's
        the real story, neither one belonging to each other.

There is a word that returns again: Realm.

I sat by a train window and traced my palm when I missed
    my mother. I was giving myself a circle, this is your palm,
        a circle which is also nature, a strangeness that is you.

What is grandeur? Who is keeping score?

I believe in the circle, in light that surprises me, when I can
    believe nothing. The palm reaching out is a gesture,
        a boundary, a circle one could slip through, or something
you could hold and in turn it could hold you back.

STARTLEMENT

It is a forgotten pleasure, the pleasure
        of the unexpected blue-bellied lizard

skittering off his sun spot rock, the flicker
        of an unknown bird by the bus stop.

To think, perhaps, we are not distinguishable
        and therefore no loneliness can exist here.

Species to species in the same blue air, smoke—
        wing flutter buzzing, a car horn coming.

So many unknown languages, to think we have
        only honored this strange human tongue.

If you sit by the riverside, you see a culmination
        of all things upstream. We know now,

we were never at the circle's center, instead
        all around us something is living or trying to live.

The world says, What we are becoming, we are
        becoming together.

The world says, One type of dream has ended
        and another has just begun.

The world says, Once we were separate,
        and now we must move in unison.

THE ORIGIN REVISITED

After a visit to the Yaak Valley in Kootenai National Forest, Montana, where the US Forest Service has announced a logging project called "Black Ram."

What is there to be done now, but enter
    against abandonment, become a hollow sound

in the halo of labyrinthine green, to become a crossed
    out word on the back of someone's hand.

Once, all of this became

    all of this. One not-yet-golden western larch
curves by a white pine, a white pine

    curves by a western hemlock, no one here
is heroic. To enter here is to enter

magnitude, to feel an ecstatic somethingness,
    a nothingness of your own name.

All words become wrong. A whole world exists
    without us. But who is us?

Lichen, moss, grizzly scat, moose hoofprint like two
    exclamation points by the drying frog pond.

How do you know you're alive? What evidence
    will you leave? So many myths

are unraveling, a yellow swallowtail glides by over
    the sinless creek bed. A storm

wets the skin and we are surprised we have
    skin. Woods' rose, white-flowered rhododendron,

nothing here is unfinished. What it gave me? I saw
    a new tree emerge out of a ground made of ancient trees

on top of more ancient trees, on top of more ancient trees,
    on top of more ancient trees, and understood then

that this was how the earth was made.

IN PRAISE OF MYSTERY: A POEM FOR EUROPA

Arching under the night sky inky
with black expansiveness, we point
to the planets we know, we

pin quick wishes on stars. From earth,
we read the sky as if it is an unerring book
of the universe, expert and evident.

Still, there are mysteries below our sky:
the whale song, the songbird singing
its call in the bough of a wind-shaken tree.

We are creatures of constant awe,
curious at beauty, at leaf and blossom,
at grief and pleasure, sun and shadow.

And it is not darkness that unites us,
not the cold distance of space, but
the offering of water, each drop of rain,

each rivulet, each pulse, each vein.
O second moon, we, too, are made
of water, of vast and beckoning seas.

We, too, are made of wonders, of great
and ordinary loves, of small invisible worlds,
of a need to call out through the dark.

NOTES ON NEW POEMS

"In the End, Everything Gives" was written in response to Andy Goldworthy's sculptural installation, *Roof,* at the National Gallery of Art.

"Startlement" was written for the front matter of the Fifth National Climate Assessment (NCA5) and was inspired by the authors of the report and their dedication to climate change awareness.

"The Origin Revisited" was written after a visit to the Yaak Valley in Kootenai National Forest, Montana, where the US Forest Service has announced a logging project called "Black Ram." My everlasting gratitude to Rick Bass for bringing me to the forest he works to protect.

"In Praise of Mystery" was written for NASA's spacecraft the *Europa Clipper*, which launched on October 14, 2024. The *Clipper* will travel to Jupiter's second moon, Europa, which scientists believe may have all the ingredients for life. The poem is engraved in my own handwriting on the vault plate of the spacecraft and was also made into a picture book by the wonderful illustrator Peter Sís.

ACKNOWLEDGMENTS FOR NEW POEMS

I have never written anything alone. Everything has been written in community, for others, with others in mind, and in conversation with all those who have written before. To those generous souls who hold me close, who read early drafts, and share their early drafts, and who give me support, love, and courage—thank you, thank you, thank you. You know who you are. I owe you everything.

I am grateful to all the hardworking editors who published these poems, sometimes in earlier versions.

"The Endlessness" appeared in *The New Yorker*.
"Hell or High Water" appeared in *The New Yorker*.
"While Everything Else Was Falling Apart" appeared in *Poetry* magazine.
"Strange Refuge" appeared in *The McNeese Review*.
"This One Goes Out To" appeared in the *Mississippi Review*.
"Mortality" appeared in *Lion's Roar*.
"Sea Turtle" appeared in *Lion's Roar*.
"Crow's-Feet" appeared in *The McNeese Review*.
"Let Loose" appeared in *Oprah Daily*.
"The Origin Revisited" appeared in *The Atlantic*.
"In Praise of Mystery" was first published on the website for the Library of Congress and NASA's *Europa Clipper* website. It was also selected to appear in *Best American Poetry*. A duplicate copy of the *Europa Clipper* vault plate where the poem is engraved is in the Library of Congress collections.

ADA LIMÓN is the author of six collections of poems, including *The Hurting Kind*, which was a finalist for the Griffin Poetry Prize; *The Carrying*, winner of the National Book Critics Circle Award and finalist for the PEN/Jean Stein Book Award; and *Bright Dead Things*, finalist for the National Book Award, the National Book Critics Circle Award, and the Kingsley Tufts Award. Limón is the recipient of a MacArthur Fellowship and a Guggenheim Fellowship and was named a 2024 *Time* Woman of the Year. She is also the author of two picture books, *In Praise of Mystery* and *And, Too, the Fox*, as well as the editor of the anthology *You Are Here: Poetry in the Natural World*. She served as the twenty-fourth Poet Laureate of the United States and lives in Glen Ellen, California.